PEACEOLOGY

For Healing Society

PEACEOLOGY

For Healing Society

ILCHI LEE

Healing Society

Healing Society, Inc.
7664 W. Lake Mead Blvd. #109
Las Vegas, NV 89128

e-mail: healingsociety@newhuman.org
Web site: www.healingsociety.org

If you are unable to order this book from your local bookseller,
you may order directly from the publisher.
Call 1-877-324-6425, toll-free.

Library of Congress Control Number: 2002110125
ISBN 0-9720282-6-9

Printed in South Korea
Book design by Pishion

Dedicated to the reader:
May you create peace.

CONTENTS

～

Author's Preface ···· *ix*
Prayer for Peace ···· *1*

PART I. WHAT IS PEACE? ···· 7
Chapter 1 **Peaceology** ···· 8
Chapter 2 **Rethinking Peace** ···· 13

PART II. WHAT IS THE PROBLEM
AND HOW DO WE FIX IT? ···· 17
Chapter 1 **Basic Principles of Peaceology** ···· 18
Chapter 2 **Realizing Peace: Recovering the
Principle of Harmony** ···· 23

PART III. FIVE STEPS FOR ACHIEVING
PEACE BY THE YEAR 2010 ···· 27
First Step **Peace through You** ···· 28
Second Step **Peace through the Brain** ···· 41
Third Step **Peace through Enlightenment** ···· 62
Fourth Step **Peace through Healing Society** ···· 84
Fifth Step **Peace through a Spiritual
United Nations (SUN)** ···· 93

Humanity Conference:
The Declaration of Humanity ···· *101*

Why Am I Writing about Peace?

⁓

I remember driving around New York City a little more than two years ago.

It was late August when the United Nations hosted the first Millennium World Peace Summit of Religious and Spiritual Leaders. More than twelve hundred of the world's preeminent religious and spiritual leaders met at the General Assembly Hall of the United Nations to discuss peace and to condemn the use of religious differences as an excuse to justify conflict and bloodshed.

New York, as it is wont to be in August, was muggy that night. Without any particular place to go, I just drove around, guided by bright lights and embraced by traffic noise that did not seem to diminish with the darkness. The lights around Times Square shone on the many people who walked the famed area, revealing the diversity of human expression more effectively than could any scientific study. Blacks walked hand-in-hand with yellows, people wearing turbans laughed along with others sporting Hashidim beards, and whites mingled with browns without a trace of self-consciousness.

Yet, despite the outer appearance of harmony, I felt an undercurrent of alienation and apathy among nationalities, races, and religions. The bright lights that revealed diversity also chased people into dark corners of buildings, and loud noises of spontaneous celebration drove people out of the streets. As I observed the scene, I thought once again, of the word peace.

Peace…peace… peace… for how long have we used this word? Of all the words in the history of humankind, no other word so embodies our highest hopes and our loftiest potential yet is, at the same time, so misunderstood and misused. So many wars and atrocities have been committed in the name of peace. So many lives have been lost in its defense.

The concept of peace probably represents the greatest example of irony in history. An ideal state of the absence of war, it has nevertheless killed so many. Belief in the right to live in accordance with individual choice has destroyed so many options. In these times, the word peace fails to arouse emotion in the hearts of most people. Yet, this word represents our highest common vision.

The world's religions have played a significant part in making a mockery of peace. Perhaps our gathering at the United Nations signals a reversal of this unfortunate fact. I had received an invitation to speak to the assembly, and I wondered what message I might send. What might I say about peace?

Peace is my life. For me, peace is the common thread connecting the beginning of the cosmos to the present, and to the future. To me, the word peace conveys the highest collective vision for humankind as well as the very essence of cosmic order.

I was born in Korea in midst of chaos and change, when the need for peace was most desperate. The year was 1950. On June 25 of that year, the well-trained and well-equipped armies of North Korea invaded a woefully unprepared South Korea along the 38th Parallel. This imaginary expanse of lush greenery, marked by an unending stretch of razor-sharp wire fence, divided North from South Korea, forcibly separating families, friends, and lovers.

For the next three years, the forces of Socialism and Capitalism clashed with all the power and fanaticism of young ideologies with a cataclysmic effect on the Korean peninsula. This eventually involved more than sixteen countries and marked the beginning of the Cold War. By its end, the war had claimed more than two million lives on both sides, including the lives of thousands of Americans.

It was in this world that I grew up, asking questions about life and death as early as I can remember, questions which led me to the long road to recognition of the true meaning of my true existence. The question, "Who am I and why am I here?" permeated my very essence and affected everything I did. In search of an answer to this question, I wandered alone through the mountainside for many nights.

I neglected family and friends in order to talk with a field of grass or a tree, hoping that nature could answer my question when human beings could not. Looking at my family and friends, I wondered how they could live so happily without knowing why they lived. Was I the only one who seemed to be suffering from an insatiable need to know the answer to this question, while others seemed to be doing fine without knowing?

I was living my life in an ordinary and superficial way when I experienced an accidental brush with the power of Ki-energy that led me to energy training. While visiting an old bookstore in the center of Seoul, I picked up a book on martial arts. Its cover was falling off. As I turned to the first page, I read a sentence that sent a jolt of electricity through me. It said, "If you achieve enlightenment through energy and positive deeds, you will be invincible." As I read that sentence, a live current ran through me and invisible warmth formed a blanket around me. I was a third degree black belt in Tae Kwon Do and had even run a school for martial arts, but I had never felt anything like it. I did not want to let go of this feeling. As I rode the bus back home, I sat huddled quietly by myself, drunk on that wonderful and powerful feeling. After that, Ki energy guided my life.

For the next one hundred days, I awoke at four o'clock in the morning and trained. I rose and climbed a hill behind my home to train and meditate for hours, without regard to time. I practiced energy breathing in order to feel and control the flow of Ki energy throughout my body and mind. I had entered into a new world. I felt my own heart beat. I felt the blood flow through my veins. Vibration coursed through my body unbidden, and I felt my body change in ways too numerous to describe.

I trained until I achieved a certain level of Ki energy. In the throes of the energy, I felt almost powerful enough to uproot trees from the ground. I felt every bone in my body disintegrate and take form again, and shook violently as Ki energy coursed through my body.

One morning, in the bitter cold, I sat in the middle of fresh snow, meditating. This was the last day of the hundred consecutive days of training I had promised myself. If I did not finish this day, I would not achieve goal. The previous ninety-nine days would have been for naught. With this in mind, I sat like a stone statute in the middle of the snow-covered field, braving the skin-biting wind. My body shook and my breathing became haggard.

Despite the obvious danger, with my determination not give up after ninety-nine days, I thought to myself, "I do not live simply because I want to, and I cannot die simply because I want to. Everything is heaven's will." My consciousness began to fade as my body began to freeze. "So this is how I am to die", I thought to myself. With effort, I let go of the last bit of myself. I fully offered myself up to heaven praying, "Because I am here by your will, you must do as you wish with my life...."

At this moment I felt my body come alive, furiously spewing out heat, melting the snow around me. I felt a powerful stream of Ki energy coursing through my body as it formed a capsule of energy to protect me from the extreme cold. This was not something I could have accomplished alone. This surge of my innermost life energy at a moment of utmost urgency and absolute trust was the ultimate experience in the power of energy, yet it felt empty.

It was empty because I was still unable to answer the simple question, "Why was I born?" Without an answer to this question, I was just a person capable of playing with energy, a mere technician, nothing more. What good was that? What good was it to know that I could survive in freezing temperatures using the power of Ki energy if I lacked the answer I had been looking for all my life?

Bemoaning my own ignorance, I returned to Moak Mountain in Central Korea and vowed not to come out until I had answers to the questions I was looking for. I decided to test my physical and mental endurance by not sleeping for twenty-one days, with only water for sustenance. I tried everything to stay awake, including sitting at the edge of a sharp cliff, my arms wrapped around the thick branch of a tree, so that the fear of falling would keep me awake. I rolled down a steep mountainside several times due to sitting on the edge of a rock in effort to keep myself from falling asleep.

Toward the end of the first week without sleep, I developed a severe headache of a magnitude I had never experienced. The pain in my eye sockets and in my ears was so severe that I could not see or hear. As time went on, my brain seemed to shrivel and begin to deteriorate. My head seemed always on the verge of exploding. After about two weeks, I knew that I would soon die. I felt a fleeting temptation to sleep, drink, and eat something in order to prolong my life a bit. I would have succumbed to temptation had I not survived the ordeal of freezing in the snow covered field.

The pain was so severe, that I knew I was beyond saving at this point. I tried to stand on my head and scream with all my might in order to relieve this pain. Eventually, I gave up. Once again, I decided to fully offer myself to the heavens above. With a loud boom, as this thought crossed my mind, I felt the world open up before me. A soothing and refreshing feeling of cool warmth enveloped me. I was beyond my body, free of pain with full clarity.

With an incredible expansion of feeling, I heard a voice cry out from deep within me, "Who am I!" The answer came... "I am Cosmic Energy". My tongue began moving of its own accord, mouthing the phrase, "My energy is Cosmic Energy, and... "My mind is the Cosmic Mind". At this moment, with profoundness that I cannot describe, I heard the sound of the universe breathing. It was the sound of my own breathing. The universe and I are not separate, but One! I am the stars, the moon, and the sun! When I see other people, I see myself. When I feel others, I am feeling myself. I became conscious that we are all sharing the same cosmic awareness. This was peace in the ultimate sense of the word, realizing that we are one with all existence.

I soon realized that this illumination or "enlightenment", for lack of a better word, carries a heavy responsibility. It is the responsibility to share this experience with others. If enlightenment benefits just one individual, what good is that enlightenment? If Truth revealed to one individual ends there, what good is that Truth? If the power of enlightenment does not change the world, it is without value, not even worth the price of a loaf of bread. I therefore, decided to test the Truth of my enlightenment by attempting to share it with the world. If my enlightenment was real, I could communicate it to others and it would affect them the way it affected me. Thus, I had found a way to express my true purpose for this life… to help others to experience the spiritual awakening of inner peace. For enlightenment is peace.

In order to do this, I realized that people must first recover physical health and energy balance, since peace must have a healthy foundation. I began by using techniques for sensitization to, and control of energy. I had learned these in the long training preceding my own spiritual awakening. From the various exercises, meditation, and martial arts that I had practiced, I devised an effective method of simple exercises designed to get people started on the road to physical, mental, and spiritual health. I called this, "Dahnhak". I systematized this program, which consists of simple stretching and breathing techniques and meditation. I began to teach it to others to help them regain physical health and emotional balance, and thereby begin to find peace.

Although Dahnhak starts out as physical exercise, its true purpose is to help people recover physical health and establish an ethical foundation for becoming a "spiritual" person who is successful in the everyday world. At the same time, Dahnhak aims not only at the spiritual enlightenment of individuals, but of society and humanity, because they cannot be separated just as individual peace and collective peace cannot be separated.

In the United States Dahnhak was honed down to its essence and gave rise to Brain Respiration, a process by which brain-power is literally used to recover health of body, mind, and spirit. In just fifteen years, the practice of Dahnhak and Brain Respiration has grown to include over one million members in more than three hundred centers in South Korea alone. There are close to ten thousand members in over fifty centers in the USA and other countries, who as Earth-Humans are joining in the Healing Society movement to create peace in their personal lives, their communities, and eventually throughout the Earth.

This movement began fifteen years ago in a local park in Korea with a single student who had partial paralysis from a stroke. At that time, I said to the student, "Although you are the only one standing in front of me, in my eyes you represent the whole of humanity." Although my grandiose statement may have surprised him, my vision was as clear then as it is now. My desire is to illustrate the Truth of my enlightenment by sharing it as widely as possible, to complete my individual peace by working to realize collective peace.

However, peace does not come about by merely wishing for it. Visions do not come true by thinking about them. We must overcome many obstacles and many difficulties. The flower of peace will blossom only when we direct all that we have toward its cause, through all manner of obstacles and difficulties.

I work for peace for completion of my own peace. To be complete, Enlightenment is must be shared. I do what I do, not for others, but for myself for ultimately I know... that I am you.

In short, I am writing about peace for my own peace of mind... and for yours.

- Ilchi Lee

Prayer of Peace

~

This prayer was written by Ilchi Lee and offered at the Opening Ceremony of the Millennium World Peace Summit of Religious and Spiritual Leaders in the General Assembly of the United Nations on August 28, 2000.

I offer this prayer of peace
Not to any one god, nor to many gods
Not to the Christian god
Nor to the Jewish god
Nor the Buddhist god
Nor the Islamic god

Not even to the indigenous gods of many nations
But to the divinity within us all
That makes us all brothers and sisters.
To make us truly One Family
In the name of humanity.

I offer this prayer of peace
To the cosmic Oneness, that is our birthright
Our privilege
And our strength
That should we let it shine forth and show us the way,
Will guide us to the road of peace.
Not the Christian peace
Not the Jewish peace
Not the Islamic peace
Nor the Buddhist peace
Not the indigenous peace of many nations
But the human peace
That has a place in the hearts of all people,
To allow us to truly fulfill our divine potential
To become children of one humanity.

I offer this prayer of peace
That we may realize
The truth of our existence
That we may discover
The sanctity of our lives
And seek

The spirituality of our beings.
Please allow us to experience
With all our hearts and our souls
The intimate connection to the divine
Which we all posses inside.
For our bodies are the temples of worship
And our souls the altars
Upon which we shall stand tall
To live out the true meaning
Of our existence.

I offer this prayer of peace
To declare a revolution
Of the human spirit.
I wish to announce that
It is now time
For all of us to spiritually awaken
To enlightenment.
That the time for an enlightened few is ended
The age of elitist enlightenment has passed.
For how long shall we seek for prophets
To come down from mountaintops
And tell us what to do?

We all must become enlightened
To recognize our divinity
To raise our consciousness
And proclaim our independence

From blind reliance on long ago sages
And draw the answers from our own well
Of spiritual wisdom.
We must ourselves become the enlightened ones.
We must ourselves realize our Oneness.
I declare that we must all become Earth-Humans
Of the earth
Not of any religion, nation, or race
But of this earth, for this earth, and by this earth
To create a lasting peace
On earth.

I offer this prayer of peace
For the United Nations
In which we stand today
To lift itself from the quicksand of politics
And live out its distinctly spiritual goal
To eradicate the disease of war
And create an equitable and peaceful world.
Let us hope that the United Nations finds
The strength and the will
To speak on behalf of all people of the earth
And not just for the few privileged nations.
Let us wish upon the United Nations the wisdom
To become the beacon that we can all follow
To the promised land of love and peace.
I pray to thee
God of all gods

Divine Spirit that lives within us
And connects us in One Life
That you grant us the vision
To establish a Spiritual United Nations
To guide us into the next millennium.

I offer this prayer of peace
With all my fellow Earth-Humans
For a lasting peace on earth.

PART 1

What Is Peace?

Chapter 1

Peaceology

~

Humankind has collectively dreamed of a peaceful world from time immemorial. Regardless of nationality, creed, ethnicity, or religious affiliation, peace is a concept that is familiar to all of us. Perhaps this is because it has been our hope for such a long time. Politicians, religious leaders and beauty contestants alike, declare peace to be the most important mission in life. Many people profess a desire for peace and many people work for peace. In the midst of war, national leaders declare that the reason for war is peace, an exercise in logical circumlocution so familiar to us that we no longer see its outrageous, inherent hypocrisy.

The Cold War divided the world into two camps in the latter half of the twentieth century. This was ostensibly about which system would create a more fair and equitable state of peaceful living. However, this only resulted in a constant threat of annihilation. Although the Cold War may be over, the world still suffers war and countless conflicts that continue to inflict deep pain on the psyche of humanity.

Undeniably, organized religion and politics remain prominent sources of conflict. Despite theology and ideology to the contrary, religious and political differences have been the mainstay of human conflict for many centuries now. Humanity has approached peace through such diverse fields as science, philosophy, politics, economics, social studies, and medicine. Yet, the true nature of peace and a solution to war remains as elusive to us as it has throughout the written history of humankind.

Perhaps the flaw is in the delegation of responsibility for peace to political and religious leaders. Perhaps instead, we need to develop a relationship between peace and individual human beings. Perhaps it is we, ourselves, who must ultimately become the actors in the drama of the creation of peace on earth.

We already know all too well that peace does not come about just because we talk about it, pray for it or subject it to modern scientific investigation. We know all too well that politicians, and religious and academic leaders cannot bring peace about by themselves. The protagonists of the drama of peace are not religions or political systems. We cannot blame politicians and religious leaders of the world for failing at the noble challenge of creating peace if it was not really their responsibility to begin with. We cannot even accuse God of neglecting the divine duty to bestow peace on Earth as it not God's lot either. The responsibility for peace lies with those of us who profess to love and want peace. In the moment of our profession, peace becomes our individual responsibility. We are all protagonists of peace. We are the leading men and women in the grand drama of peace.

If you want to lead a happy life, it is up to you to create this for yourself. Likewise, if you want a peaceful life, then you have to create peace. Peace is not an errand that you can ask others to run for you. If you want to earn respect as a human being and to conclude this life proudly as the universal spiritual being, that you are, then you have no choice. You must know peace and realize it in your own life, as it is only possible to sustain integrity and sanctity of human life on a stage of peace. To know and express peace in every action of everyday life, is the most basic of duty of those who profess peace.

What is peace? Does humanity really want peace? What is the reality of the peace we are pursuing? What is the purpose of peace and what is the good it will it bring? Who is the bene-factor of peace and who is the beneficiary of peace? How can we overcome the divisions and conflicts that plague life on Earth today? How can we bring into reality politics for peace, religion for peace, and economics for peace? What is the way to actualize peace in every experience in health, education, and culture?

In this book I wish to speak of everything I know, understand, and feel about peace. It is my sincere hope that many people will agree with what I say and join me in a movement to heal society and establish peace on Earth. For only by our efforts at healing and peace, will the collective human consciousness make the next evolutionary leap forward, and allow us to continue the divine journey to the completion and perfection of our human souls.

This is not an academic tome. I do not wish to analyze peace by conventional academic methods. There have been many upon many academic studies done on peace already, with very little result in the actual production of peace. Peace is ultimately a human issue. If you do not understand the reality of who you are as a human being, you will be chasing false shadows of peace for the rest of your life. Before our social and political systems can change, humans must change. Not one or two people, but enough people to create a culturally significant and lasting impact on the course of universal human experience in the future. This is the goal of the Healing Society movement. I am working to make spiritual enlightenment common sense. This will lead to peace.

Peace is a matter of application, rather than theory. It is a mistake to think we are contributing to peace on Earth just because we think, speak, or give lectures about peace. We cannot actualize peace with words and thoughts alone. We can bring peace to the world only by concrete and sustained effort to heal body, mind, and spirit for ourselves, our neighbors, our communities, and for the whole of humanity. My intention is to provide philosophical underpinnings, actual plans for action, and a detailed vision for achieving lasting and equitable peace on Earth. This is the agenda for Peaceology.

Peaceology, a new philosophy and application for peace, must become the new spring from which our collective human soul draws the water of spiritual life. Peaceology must become the standard bearer of a new definition of health. Peaceology must become the rallying cry for a new generation of social and cultural activists. Peaceology is a system centered not on one specific nation, religion, or cultural tradition... but on the Earth herself. Peaceology is not for experts, but for everyone who wants a peaceful world for humanity. Peaceology does not contain difficult concepts or theories. Peaceology simply offers common sense ideas and actions for those of us who would prefer to live in a world of peace... an earth centered peace to restore health and beauty to humanity and the earth.

Chapter 2

Rethinking Peace

~

What is peace? Do we really want peace? Why do we need peace?

Although these questions seem rhetorical or idiotic in their simplicity, a universal definition of peace with which to answer them does not actually exist. Peace is an easy word to bandy about, but it is difficult to pin down it's meaning. We need a definition of peace that addresses the needs of the whole world and in which everyone has an interest. What could be the reason for our failure to achieve peace when so many have clamored for it throughout the ages? Perhaps, in part, it is because we do not know exactly what peace is, or that what we think is peace, is not actually peace.

Until now, resolution of the issue of peace has considered too large for an individual to tackle. Individual efforts would surely not have any bearing on peace, anyway... or so we thought. Yet, peace determined by prevailing political ideology or religious dogma, is bound to be imperfect and temporary. Eventually, a more powerful force behind a different ideology will rise to challenge such peace. In fact historically, peace based on prevailing values of nation or religion has inevitably led to further conflict and bloodshed, rather than a to lasting state of peace

Lack of peace has remained an albatross around our collective necks. Peace remains a distant goal that we are forever bound to pursue yet not attain. We are subject to the whims of powerful and cynical leaders who use our universal longing for personal gain. Peace has become something unapproachable and abstract, moving farther from our grasp.

What we now need is not an intellectual understanding of peace. What we really need now is for all of us to become more peaceful, to ourselves become expression of peace. This can only happen when we undergo a fundamental and profound experience of peace. Until you personally experience the infinite depth of peace within yourself, how can you expect to exist peacefully for yourself and others?

Peace is Breathing

Peace is not an abstract concept. Peace is the nature of our very lives. The most basic function of our lives, the breath, is peace incarnate. What would happen if you stopped breathing for even one minute? Would you feel peaceful? How would you feel if you were able to breathe in but could not breathe out? What would happen if you could eat as much as you wanted to eat, but could not excrete, or drink as much as you wanted to drink but you could not urinate? If you have ever suffered from severe constipation, you know how uncomfortable you would be. This is why I say peace is like breathing. Peace is a natural and uninterrupted rhythm of life.

The breathing cycle illustrates the balance and rhythm of life. Oxygen enters the body and our lungs expell carbon dioxide by breathing. Without circulation of breath, we cannot maintain life. The basic bodily functions that maintain life all consist of complete cycles. Simply put, a never-ending cycle of energy and material makes our lives possible.

Breath has it own rhythm. Breathing in itself, is a perfect self-balancing mechanism of life, becoming faster or slower depending on conditions. It goes out just as it came in. You cannot maintain life if you foolishly try to prevent your breath from leaving, or stop air from coming in to begin with. Breathing is a fair and exact transaction. Life consists of a series of balanced and precise cycles. Peace is like the orderly and harmonious rhythm of life. Peace is the healthy functioning of the rhythms and cycles of life.

Peace is instinctive to humans, the essence of the rhythm of life. It is the eternal immutable law of the cosmos. Peace is part of our human nature. It is as natural and instinctive as breathing. Again, hold your breath for two minutes and see how you feel. Think about how long we have been without peace. If someone looked down at the collective human face, it would be blue. The absence peace is not natural. If we apply the principles of harmonious rhythm to society, it will inevitably become more peaceful. This book suggests that we apply the natural rhythms of life to human society, in everyday thoughts and actions.

PART 2

What Is the Problem and How Do We Fix It?

Chapter 1

Basic Rules of Peaceology

~

Peace is the healthy and harmonious order of life. The
nucleus of this order consists of two factors: an
unchangeable central point and a set of rules that governs
movement around the center. Only when all of the various
parts of a system agree upon a center and move according to
a certain set of rules, is total and comprehensive order
possible. For this to happen, this center must be a point on
which all elements of the system agree. It must have
unanimous appeal and universal meaning of greater impor-
tance than the differences inevitable to any system.
Furthermore, the rules that govern the separate elements of

the system must be fair and consistent and must be essential to the co-existence and co-operation of the system. Only then will all the different elements of a system accept the rules willingly and co-create a healthy and harmonious order that will, in turn, benefit all elements of the system.

The three basic rules needed for creation of a system of harmonious order are as follows: Revolution vs. Rotation, Centripetal vs. Centrifugal Force, and Fairness vs. Equality. These three "rules" provide not only the principle underpinnings of a harmonious order but also strength to maintain it. In short, these are rules for peace. The reason the human body works so well, is that the body operates according to these rules.

Rule One, *Revolution vs. Rotation.* The Earth rotates on its own axis while revolving around the sun. As in all of these rules, the order of the descriptive terms is crucial. Rotation must not come first, or at the expense of revolution. Likewise, you cannot put your own self-interest in front of the collective good. In this case, if revolution itself stops, the result will be an abrupt halt in rotation. In other words, self-destruction will occur. If the order of the solar system were to break down, the Earth could not exist its own. Individual action that does not add constructively to movement of the whole is bound cause trouble. When our consciousness is in synchronicity with the process of collective revolution, we will judge the desirability of our individual actions by first consulting a standard for collective good, and abide by the rules of harmonious living.

Rule Two, *Centripetal vs. Centrifugal Force.* As an object rotates around a central axis, the force that pulls the object toward the center, keeping it in a stable orbit, is centripetal force. This is basic high school physics. Imagine you are swinging a sling whose pouch contains a rock, above your head. Your arm provides the centripetal force that keeps the rock from flying off into the air. The rock's tendency to fly off at every turn is the centrifugal force. A combination of the centripetal and centrifugal forces keeps the rock in proper orbit, balanced, potential constructive energy.

Centrifugal force, the individual, must not become stronger than the centripetal force, or community, or it will destroy the balance and the individual will fly off into oblivion. Centripetal force without its centrifugal counterpart is a mere possibility, without real force. Conversely, centrifugal force without centripetal counterbalance is a destructive and unbalancing force. Only when balance between the forces is stable is the overall movement of the system similarly stable.

Rule Three, *Fairness vs. Equality.* Systemic balance depends on fair judgment of the various differences within a system. Fairness must come before equality, for the reverse of this breeds resentment and contempt, leading to apathy and inaction. The old Soviet system is an example of this. A fair judgment of the differences in ability, production, and circumstances is prerequisite to equitable balance within a community. Otherwise, it is the same as giving the identical amount of food to both a child and a grown adult and expecting them both to do the same of work. Not only will this waste food, it will also create unrealistic expectations that are bound to fail. Therefore, fairness must precede equality. In society, fairness and equality represent a clear delineation of roles and responsibility for one's actions, followed by fair judgment of the achievement of individuals.

With faithful adherence to these rules, whole systems will run smoothly regardless of size, from the nuclear family to the multi-national conglomerate, to the universe itself. Without maintaining synchronistic orbit by working with the center, we will collide with others. If we do not maintain velocity to sustain balance of multidirectional forces, we will fly off into oblivion. Without a fair way to judge inevitable differences in ability, productivity, and circumstances, we will not be able to maintain balance and harmony in a given system.

The human body is a prime example of this. Each cell has a set of infinite possibilities to choose from, for it contains a complete set of information to become anything in the human body. However, cells align with the needs of the whole organism. External force does not impose order on our body. Rather it is an example of a self-organizing and self-maintaining bio-order. It truly is a miracle. This is only possible because each cell follows the three rules discussed above. This is why the phenomenon of life is so precious and beautiful in its expression of harmonious order. No cell can exist without first considering the entire organism. No individual should exist without thinking first of society. Similarly, humanity cannot exist without first thinking of the system of life that is the Earth. Such is the basic principle of harmonious order. This is the basic principle of peace.

Chapter 2

Realizing Peace: Recovering the Principle of Harmonious Living

~

The crisis that we are facing today stems from our failure to adhere to the three rules of peace. A devastating result of this is our tendency to see everything in parts, to divide everything into "me" and the rest of the world. Another tragic result of disregard for these rules is the prevalence of human selfishness and egotism. This is none other than the proverbial "fall from grace" or expulsion from the Garden of Eden.

The concepts of "the fall from grace" and "moral corruption" denote none other than our disrespect for the rules of harmonious order and peace. Original Sin refers not to Adam and Eve's eating of the fruit of the Tree of Knowledge, but to our forgetfulness regarding the rules of harmony and order that run the universe and all of life. Selfishness and egotism are direct evidence of our collective divine fall. Our disregard for the rules of harmonious order has led us directly to the current crisis, or lack of peace. This is nothing less than a crisis of human identity and of human survival.

If our fall from divine grace is the result of our disregard for the rules of harmonious order, then we can expect recovery of our true nature to begin when follow them once again. However, recovering our capacity to observe the rules will not happen without effort on our part. This is a matter of intellect, understanding, and awareness, by individual and collective choice.

Peace will not occur magically because one or two individuals awaken to the truth of the nature of harmony and order. Peace will only prosper when the principle of harmonious order becomes common sense, rather than a novel idea. Therefore, Peaceology suggests that the solution lies in education in all its forms, for unless there is a fundamental change in human beings, changes in government and social policy will have little effect. This is why I say in my book Healing Society, that enlightenment is the answer for building a peaceful world.

I believe we must begin to teach a new world-view in simple terms. We must emphasize development of character and responsible action based on the three basic laws of harmony. We must teach that enlightenment is common sense within the grasp of all. Then these ideas will translate a new system of living peace.

Enlightenment means recognizing the harmonious rhythm of nature within each of us, and thus the true meaning of peace. Enlightenment means understanding that our shared reality is not the physical body or personal character, but inner divinity, conscience, and soul. It is the realization that we are a manifestation of universal harmony itself. Enlightenment is peace. Enlightenment is a choice. Therefore, peace is also a choice.

Since it is intangible, the only evidence of enlightenment is the change in our thoughts and actions. Enlightenment without action is meaningless. Enlightenment only matters when the principles of harmony and natural order become the basis for thoughts and actions expressed in the real world. Then personal desires will take a back seat to the collective good.

What fundamental change does enlightenment bring to our thinking and behavior? First, our life's goal will shift from single-minded focus on material success to a desire to move toward completion or perfection. Second, control will no longer be the underlying basis of all human relationships. Mutual respect will stand in place of control. Third, the basis for our transactions will change from competition to cooperation. Fourth, our concept of ownership will change from that of possession to that of stewardship. Fifth, our concept of profit will shift to public benefit from personal gain. The basis for a society that considers enlightenment a matter of common sense, is the principles of harmonious living.

When all have recovered the principle of harmony, we will

have peace. When all awaken to their true peaceful human nature and adhere to the principles of harmonious living, self-interest will no longer be socially acceptable. Selfishness can exist in society only when others do not recognize it as being unreasonable. When we no longer tolerate selfishness, a peaceful collective conscience will prevail. This will give rise to a culture of harmony.

PART 3

*Five Steps to Peace
by 2010*

First Step

Peace through You

≈

Why have we strayed so far from peace? In order to realize peace on earth, we need someone to take peace by hand and plant it in the ground. Who will it be? When we all wish to be beneficiaries of peace, who then will be the benefactor of peace? Who will be the creator of peace?

Generally, we think that peace is a concept too abstract and remote to have any bearing on our personal lives. When someone answers that his highest hope or dream is for world peace, we are skeptical, and may think he is being facetious. We think that peace is matter for politics and religion, outside of our own realm of experience.

When people speak publicly of world peace or of curing social ills of humanity, they tend to be people with high visibility. When such influential people talk about peace and human welfare, we tend to nod at their words of wisdom. However, nine out of ten times, their talk of peace contains a personal agenda.

Most business people are primarily interested in making money. When a person talks about peace in the context of business, we wonder whether he is using peace as a marketing ploy. There is an easy way to find out, however. Ask if he or she would be willing to take a profit loss or forgo a lucrative deal in the interest of world peace.

The same goes for a politician. The primary goal of a politician is to attain and maintain power. When a politician speaks of peace, he may be using it as an issue to keep his grip on power. Ask him whether he would be willing to relinquish his power in order to facilitate world peace, then you will see his true intentions. The primary job of a military officer is to win a war. When he justifies killing with rhetoric of peace, ask him whether he would willing to surrender a battle or lose the war in the interest of peace.

The divine mission of a religious leader is to bring more people to his particular faith. Ask him whether he would be willing to forsake his religion for world peace and you will know of his true will. Similarly, celebrities focus mainly on expanding popularity. Ask if they would accept anonymity for world peace. If not, when a celebrity speaks of peace, he is using it as a tool to gain popularity and fame.

For many of these people, peace is not an end, but a means to personal gain, without any real bearing on world peace. Of course, I am not discounting the people who are willing to give their best in the interest of world peace. Though I am perhaps a bit cynical, peace will not come out of blind naiveté. Peace will come about only by the conscious choice of fully informed and determined people who are masters of their own brains.

Many people continue to exploit the issue of peace for many reasons. Yet, peace seems farther and father away from our immediate realm of experience. A wall of experts has made the choice for peace inaccessible to most of us. We have surrendered our inherent right to, and responsibility for peace.

When I point my index finger to the ceiling, unless there is a problem with your vision, or you are predisposed to see more than one finger, you will see one finger. If you turn this eye on the world today, you will see what I have just described. The amazing thing is that we have ignored such obvious hypocrisy and doubletalk for such along time. Who then, will be the protagonists of peace? Who will actualize peace on Earth?

Peace will not occur as the result of rhetoric by people who exploit the idea as a means to some other end. Peace will be the result of the effort of people who see peace as the end. Their ultimate goal is peace, and their means must be peaceful. Peace will not be the result of a triumphant biblical battle against dark, mythical forces of evil. The ways and means used to bring about peace on Earth must be of the same peace they seek to realize.

Therefore, what we need to know now, is how we ourselves can become an expression of peace. As we experience peace and become peaceful, peace will prevail. When you experience peace within yourself, and develop full confidence in the power of this peace, you will communicate it to others.

You are the Creator of Peace

Peace, like our breath, exists very comfortably and very close to us. Peace is our very breath and life. This is why anyone can discover peace and help to bring it about. Peace is everyone's purpose in life, not the province of a few select individuals. It is not something that a select group of politicians, artists, or even religious leaders can do for us. You and I, one individual at a time, are all creators and benefactors of peace, as well as its beneficiaries. Until now, responsibility for peace fell to people of influence. Now we must reclaim our own responsibility and right to peace. Those who truly love humanity, the Earth, and peace are experts in peace. One who truly loves life is a specialist in peace.

The first step toward peace is to realize that you yourself are the creator and benefactor of peace. You have a responsibility to change the unsustainable direction of current civilization, and you have the power to change the direction humanity toward peace.

From Inhaling to Exhaling

Breath is the most natural and immediate expression of life. Inhaling and exhaling, expansion and contraction… this rhythmic cycle maintains its specific and mystical order even in midst of disorder. Breath is the epitome of perfect balance, cycle, and rhythm. It is fortunate that we do not have to consciously control our own breathing, for we would not be able to sleep, eat, or do anything else. However, without our effort, we breathe naturally and without fail, as long as there is life. This is an immediate example of the natural order of the cosmos and an intimate example of the love of the Creator.

The Korean term for this rhythm of life is Yullyo. Although today, Yullyo is also a musical term to denote harmony of contrasting notes, it originally described the rhythm of the cosmos, the source of universal harmony. Yullyo is the underlying principle and original energy of the universe expressed through light, sound, and vibration. Yullyo is nothing less than Cosmic Energy and Cosmic Mind.

There are countless manifestations of this endless rhythm of life. Pounding waves, curving of mountaintops, and breasts, infinity figures, the geometric representations of our own brain waves, and the brain waves themselves, the shapes of leafs, and the forms of fish are all living examples of this rhythm.

Consciously or unconsciously, we follow the rhythm of breathing faithfully. In accordance with the laws of breathing, we must exhale in order to inhale, or contract in order to expand again. We can fill up again when we have emptied ourselves. Life moves with natural rhythms and cycles of the universe. Our breath, our heart beat, all our crucial life functions follow this rhythm without fail. Our lives are an essential part of the rhythm of Yullyo.

The life of an individual, the life of a nation, and the life of each species moves according to this rhythm. How well and healthy an organism's life is, depends on how well and harmoniously the organism maintains this rhythm. This goes for an entire nation as well as the whole of humanity. On an individual level, we are healthy in body and mind when we adhere to the laws of breathing. On a larger plane, all of society will be in harmony when this rhythm is collectively recognized and maintained.

Unfortunately however, our current way of living is not following this the most basic law of life. Let us see what our current civilization teaches us to pursue and what it considers growth or maturity. When we equate ourselves with our physical bodies, and consider our consciousness to consist merely of the knowledge and information that we have injested since our birth, we are unaware of our true place as a grand expression of the cosmos. Then we have no choice perhaps, but to pursue goals that are external and material.

The desire to possess and control, govern the drive to pursue external goals. With these, competition, victory, and defeat are inevitable. The need to win far exceeds that which can be possessed or controlled. More and more people are fighting for smaller and smaller pieces of the pie. Competition cannot satisfy everyone, for it is a system of separating the players into winners and losers. For every winner there is a loser, for every success a failure, and for every feeling of happiness, a sense of despair. This creates a pool of losers filled with insecurity and fear. Eventually this results in violence, creating even more victims to perpetuate further violence.

The harder we pursue the goals set by our material civilization, the more we destroy our own ecosystem, deplete our resources, pollute our air, and lay barren mental and spiritual richness. Our material civilization is ever growing and becoming more complicated. When a system gets too large, its efficiency decreases dramatically, requiring more and more energy to maintain less and less of the system. Ironically, we call this process, "growth."

Since such "growth" destroys the very platform it rests on, it is bound to self-destruct. We are riding on a bicycle that we cannot stop pedaling because if we stop, we will fall. Although we know that we are heading toward a cliff, we cannot stop for fear of falling and skinning our knees. In spite of knowing that our demise is imminent, we cannot stop this process of endless competition for the thing called the "growth." We are breathing in only, without breathing out. If we continue to pursue only external goals without pausing to breathe out, we will surely be history ourselves in the near future.

Change of Direction

The results of the direction of our civilization are now visible in our dying ecosystems, depleted resources, over population, impoverished culture, and diminishing unity of collective will... all major indicators of healthy civilization. Something is wrong. The term, "non-sustainable" applies here and now, not only to the crisis of the environment, but to the crises of peace, human dignity, and even human survival.

Humanity is at a critical point in the material civilization. No one and nothing can exist for long without completing the natural cycle of life. Nothing can exist without breathing out before breathing in again. This rule applies to individuals and to civilizations. It applies to the earth and the universe. To prevent our civilization from running headlong into an abrupt and spectacular end, we must at least stop inhaling. We have reached our lung capacity.

In order to continue this grand cycle of life, we must soon begin to exhale... exhale quickly or slowly, but exhale! After that we can we breathe in again. We have to realize the wisdom of simple breathing. The choice is before us. For the very survival of humanity, we need to collectively let our breath out.

We need a profound shift in the direction of our civilization. We need to breathe a worldwide sigh of relief. Instead of an army of experts who see separate parts of the picture, we need to be enlightened enough to see the whole picture, with the wisdom to complete the cycles of life, so that we may begin again.

Make no mistake… breathing out will require nothing less than a fundamental change in our system of living, our ideas about ourselves, the social values that govern our desires, our entire cultural system, and ultimately, the direction of the human civilization.

Duality

An underlying philosophy of duality, which sees the self and the world as disparate and separate parts, is at the root of our material civilization. Heaven and earth, mind and body, subject and object, god and man, you and me, nature and civilization, good and evil, black and white, yin and yang…. Whether you are from the East or the West, these dichotomies are part of the world we live.

In such a world, you have to die so that I might live. It is a matter of you or me. There is no space for you and me. Since we define society and the world in this way, I must conquer you in order to save me and decrease your lot to increase mine. Confrontation, domination, competition, opposition… these are driving forces of dualistic thinking. The result of this is a lack of peace.

The History of Gods

Prime examples of duality are the organized religions of the world. Confrontation over their respective gods has led to unending bloodshed and suffering, which we need not go into deeply here. It is ironic that loving and merciful gods have been the source of so much violence and bloodshed. The fact that we do not share an awareness of this inherent contradiction is one of the bigger mysteries of the human condition. Until we address this contradiction, we cannot bring peace into this world. Without reconciliation among gods and religions, peace is impossible.

In order to overcome the problem of different gods, we need a higher divine entity. Who could bring all these omniscient and omnipotent gods together for a round of negotiation and reconciliation? Ultimately, the responsibility lies with human beings. It is up to us to require gods of love, to love, gods of peace to be peaceful, and gods of mercy to exercise mercy. When there is peace on Earth, our gods will become peaceful. When we exercise love in the world, our gods will become gods of love.

Let us examine our relationship to our gods. First, lets look at the "god-centered" Age of Faith. In this age, god(s) became the center of our world, controlling everything from plants and animals to floods and lighting. We were at the constant mercy of this god. Gods that rose to prominence during this period shared several general characteristics. Chief among them, were selfishness, possessiveness, immature display of anger and sexual conquest, and often cruelty, administered by severe punishment.

All gods seem to have their favorite nations or peoples, toward whom they direct their favor. These nation or ethnic-centered gods represent the collective identity and ego of a particular group or organization. The fact that we are still engaged in religious conflict speaks to the essentially prejudicial nature of our current gods. We do not have a god that can represent the whole Earth. The god-centered age is therefore an era of immaturity of the human spirit. Academics generally agree that god-centered world gradually gave way to modern science and humanistic philosophy of the seventeenth century, though its influence is still pervasive.

Humanism began with the Renaissance and the Age of Science and Reason, opening our eyes to the power and potential of the human intellect. We can refer to this as a human centered time, which continues to this day, as the Rational Age. In this age, humanity has acquired technical skills, and information that we could not previously have imagined. Unfortunately, with advancement in technology, we have become a threatening entity to all life and to the Earth herself. Most of us are still drunk on the success of human civilization, wreckage strewn along the path of achievement. This is evidence that the Human-Centered Age, like the God-Centered Age before it, is still imperfect and immature.

God-Human Centered Age

With the awakening of a collective human consciousness, a new age will begin. This will be the God-Human Age, or the Age of Enlightenment. In the Chinese ideogram, which for East Asian languages, is akin to the Latin roots of western languages, this sounds very eloquent and translates directly to "Deus-Homo- Unitas-Mono", or "God-Human-United-One".

The crucial part of collective spiritual awakening is for each human being to recognize that he or she is a spiritual being. By discovering the divinity within each of us, we will bridge the gap between our gods and ourselves. We will develop a new identity… a fusion of god and human, divinity and humanity. When we realize that the divinity within is none other than our soul, peace, and love, we will eradicate barriers of regional and ethnic gods. We will welcome a new Age of Human Divinity, powered by innate human spirituality and conscience. We will no longer live in an age of god-worship, but one of god-use, in which we use the "god-ness" within to effect peace and love in the world.

The term "god" commonly refers to two things. First, the term "god" denotes the preconceptions and legends of a particular tradition of faith. This use of the word "god," in Korean tradition can mean "ghost" in the Western sense. This word then refers to the phenomenon of possession, when a stray ghost forcibly pushes the rightful master of a person's consciousness out, and becomes the de-facto master. This is not a movie script or a remnant of past superstition. We suffer possession right now. We have created volumes of information… preconceptions, prejudices and justifications that have become our gods. We have freely allowed these to enter and take over our bodies, brains, and energy. Worse, we claim loyalty when we kill or die for the sake of our false masters. Such gods are no more than malicious ghosts.

The second sense in which we use the word "god" is to describe ultimate reality that exists of, and in, itself. Our inner divinity is the divinity of life, expressed as harmony of rhythm and cycle. In this sense, god does not seek to dominate or become an object of worship. This god is the principle of harmony that allows us to discover the true value of life and express our own version of joyful order in the world. We may call this god, Original Mover, Blissful Emptiness, Cosmic Energy, or Cosmic Mind. This god is beyond the realm of existence and yet, united with all existence. This is the God of Peace and Harmony.

If we really want peace, we need to use peace as the yardstick by which we measure our various gods. What kind of help can gods created by specific groups of people to justify their own ends, offer us? What type of healing can they bestow upon the world? How can they help us recover lost health and harmony? We will not have peace until we collectively recognize our prejudice and share mastership of our world.

Peace through the Power Brain

~

The brain is the key to peace. Who is the current master of your brain? Who is controlling your thoughts and actions? What is making you to think, feel, and act as you are at this moment?

The question, "Who is the master of your brain?" may sound more than a little offbeat and strange, but it is a sad truth that many people have given up mastership of their own brains. Use of your brain does not only mean activating a percentage of brain cells for your intellectual activities.

It is the more fundamental issue of the true nature of the primary mover of your brain. We are unaware of how much of

our original consciousness has been clouded over by precon-
ception and prejudice disguised as information. This is similar
to wearing colored glasses for so long that we forget we are
wearing them think the tinted colors we see are the real, true
colors. It is this information that makes us laugh, cry, swear or
lash out with anger. Our preconceptions predispose us toward
certain emotional reactions, which in turn trigger certain
thought patterns that we express in actions. When these
actions persist, they become ingrained habits, which form our
personality and which eventually determine our life's destiny.

Faced with an identical situation, people with different
preconceptions respond in different ways. Although basic
human emotions have their root in physiology of the brain, we
all act differently, depending on the information in our brains.
This is the information that pervades human civilization and
that we receive from the moment we are born. Depending on
whether your reaction is to like or dislike certain people,
things, or situations, your thought process determines whether
you become involved or move farther away from them. Your
thoughts generate your actions. Thoughts and emotional
reactions perpetuate each other, and information inside your
brain predetermines both thoughts and emotions. Once again,
who then is the master of your brain?

Everyone has a brain. However, not many of us live our
lives as masters of our own brains. We allow others to run our
brains for us with the information we receive. Our brain
begins to receive information manufactured by others from

the moment of birth. This starts with our parents and their preconceptions of the world, which soon became our preconceptions. In school, our brains were under the influence of teachers. In church, it was the preachers and in temples, our brains were the domain of bronzes or rabbies. It is very difficult to assess which information is good for us and external information controls our brains.

When you are not the master of your own brain, preconceptions become the master. For the most part, you have not chosen this information. You have never chosen to be subject to these daily doses of information. They have come in without any explicit permission on your part and are now acting the part of master of the house. This happened because you did not realize that you were the actual master of the house. Now, in order to regain control of your house, you need to understand where this information came from in the first place.

The information most deeply rooted in our being has to do with our sense of country and religion. However, without looking at our own brain objectively, we never realize that who we think we are, is the result information based on where we were born, the religion of our parents, the size of our family, the language we speak, our education, and so forth. Unless we realize that we far exceed this accumulation of information, we will never find out whom we truly are. We will always identify with being American, Korean, or Chinese. We will be Christian, Catholic, or Muslim. We will be fat or thin, smart or not. Trapped in information that has defined us since birth, we never had a chance to recognize that we have a much greater identity. We do not realize that we are Earth-Humans, born to the Earth.

Unless we awaken to our identity as spiritual beings, we will always let information received from others rule our brain and thereby, our thoughts and actions. We will allow political ideologies, religious dogma, and cultural preconceptions to determine who we think we are. This is like leaving your computer on, and having someone else come in and program it without your permission.

It is now time for you to reclaim your brain. You must be able to clearly see what types of information reside in your brain and with what effect. Then ask yourself whether this is what you want. Do you want to do the work of peace? Do you want to heal, or do you want to kill? Then, is the information inside your brain appropriate for the work you want to do? If not, who put that information inside your brain for what purpose? What is making you think others could be your enemy?

The time has come for us to comprehensively examine our brains and do a spring-cleaning, if we must. We have an inherent right to do housekeeping on our own house. Let us chase the false masters away, reclaim our own power. Let us allow our own souls to become the master of our brains and use it for creative and peaceful purposes.

The Key to Peace: the Human Brain

Human beings are ultimately the key to world peace. The brain controls human beings and determines the value of human life and peace. Information is what controls the brain. The brain feeds on information as it observes, analyzes, judges, and commands, generating more information in its turn. The brain even needs information to see. If you did not have information about what flowers look like, do you think you would "see" one even if you were looking right at one? How can you know the sound of a bird if your brain contains no information about what a bird sounds like? Therefore, the worth of a brain depends on the quantity and quality of information it contains. You can determine how good a brain is by the type of information it generates.

We sometimes confuse the level of our awareness with the level of our intellect. Just because a person can easily understand obtuse or difficult material does not mean that he has a high level of consciousness or awareness. A brain that possesses a high level of awareness is one that can produce bright, healthy, and positive information. No matter how high the IQ might be, if a brain produces information that induces negativity and darkness in others, his brain is dark. When bright brains gather to produce bright information, a healthy society will form.

The brain is a blank slate when we are born. Then it forms a shell of preconceptions and prejudices. The shell eventually grows thick enough to hide our true nature, our soul, from the world, creating an identity that is not our true self, but a false self. Since the false self is a fabrication, it cannot be complete or perfect, leading always to self-doubt and anxiety. It is dependent on the equally imperfect information provided by government and religion. A brain inside the shell of a false self can no longer hear the voice of the true self, as it acts in the selfish interest of the false self. Such a brain produces dark and negative information, ultimately contributing to the demise of the self and its surroundings.

When you become the master of your own brain by awakening to your soul, you can use your brain to its fullest capacity, and become the master of your own life. You will be able to select the information that goes into your brain, protect your brain from harmful or negative information, and generate information that will heal yourself and your neighbors and affect society positively. A spiritually awakened brain is a Power Brain, capable of listening to the divinity within, living according to the conscience of the soul, and producing positive information that will brighten the world and heal society. This kind of brain holds the key to peace. This brain will be our most powerful tool for peace.

Brain with Power

The quickest way to discover peace within and to project that peace outward is to awaken your brain, have a conversation with it, and activate its full potential. The reason that

Peaceology emphasizes the brain so much is that peace depends on the human brain. The way for your brain to become a powerful tool for peace is to develop it into a Power Brain.

A Power Brain is a creative brain. A creative brain has bright imagination and is flexible enough to accommodate many diverse ideas. A Power Brain will not give in to the despair of present adversity, but will use its bright imagination to picture a bright future. A creative brain can find a solution to any problem it faces on the journey to peace.

A Power Brain is a peaceful brain. A Power Brain knows that its true nature is peace, and considers peace its highest value, using it to measure everything else. A peaceful brain understands the principle of harmonious living and adheres to the rules of harmonious order. A peaceful brain produces positive information that will help actualize peace on Earth. A peaceful brain generates healing information.

A Power Brain is a productive brain. A productive brain is not lazy, is always responsible and realistic. A productive brain is a brain that can achieve real gains in this world for the purpose of peace. A productive brain utilizes all resources at its disposal efficiently and without waste, finishing all tasks cleanly and completely. A productive brain has the ability to become a CEO of peace.

Equation of Peace

Recent terrorist attacks have taught us how fragile the foundation of what we call peace really is. Furthermore, we found out that we cannot guarantee peace with military might or wealth. Threats to peace lurk in every corner. Peace will not result from increased military spending or more missiles. Conversely, the false sense of superiority and confidence generated by increased military strength might push us further from peace.

On the other hand, we will not have peace just because we pray or meditate for hours on end. Peace will not happen just because good people invest their precious time in good works. Peace is not so easy that it will materialize because we devote time and money, despite all the good intentions of the world.

Peace will not occur by individual good will and deeds but by organized, realistic, and concrete power. Peace is the largest project and the grandest business in the history of humankind. It can only become successful with every ounce of time, energy, and ability of all people who consider peace the highest value in their lives. This will form the backbone of the power of peace.

The equation of peace below is an attempt to represent this power of peace in a mathematical format. It is as follows:

$P = EN^2$, where

    P = the Power of Peace

    E = Enlightenment (or level of collective human
        awareness)

    N= the number of enlightened and peaceful
        people, also known as New Humans

P is the power that can actualize peace on Earth in the real sense. E is the level of enlightened awareness and its vision of peace. Vision for peace emerges naturally out of enlightened awareness, and provides a purpose or goal for a Power Brain. N is the number of New Humans, or people who have enlightened awareness, and consequently engage willingly in the grand project for peace. New Humans have genuine love for humanity, which gives rise to their desire for peace, and the desire to devote their time, effort, abilities, and resources to the cause of peace. In another words, N also represents the number of Power Brains in the world.

Power of Peace directly correlates not to the number of New Humans, but to the number of New Humans raised to the power of two. According to the rules of harmonious living, enlightened awareness will touch at least one other person, awakening of power of his or her healing energy. These people will work for peace, and they will inspire at least one other person to join in. Therefore, two New Humans will instigate four Power Brains. These will in turn, give rise to additional Power Brains. When there are one hundred million Power Brains in the world, the combined power for peace will change the future of humanity and the Earth.

Creating a Power Brain

We know that a Power Brain can be a primary catalyst for peace. Then how do you train your brain to become one? I call the method that I have devised and taught to millions of people throughout the world for the last twenty years Brain Respiration. Brain Respiration is a comprehensive and systematic method of developing potential of your brain so that it becomes a Power Brain.

The human brain is the nexus where the mind and the body meet. Energy is the medium through which the mind and body communicate, just as electricity connects software and hardware that together run a computer. Brain Respiration trains the brain by using three interrelated and distinct elements: material, energy, and spirit.

Material, energy, and spirit are the basic elements that constitute the human body and human existence itself. Since we exist in a world defined by the five physical senses, we often do not recognize the energetic and spiritual aspects of life. All we recognize is the material phenomena, and we call this the physical body.

We have three bodies. The first is the physical body perceived by the five senses. When our bodies are supremely relaxed yet our awareness alert, we can feel an energy field that surrounds our bodies. This energy field permeates and envelops us. Some people can actually see this field of energy. This is the energy body. The third body is the spiritual body.

The five senses cannot observe the spiritual body. We cannot touch, smell, see, or feel the spirit. Our existence on the material plane is a phenomenon of various aspects of our spirit expressed in this particular time and space. Information itself is not subject to the limitations of time or space. Absolute freedom, infinite existence... these terms refer to the realm of the spirit.

The highest level of activity in the phenomenon of life is "information generation." When we create or generate information, then material substance comes into being to actualize that information. The spiritual body consists of pure information. In fact, the spiritual body is synonymous, in a way, to the "information body." An example could be this book, a dance or a musical performance, building a house or inventing a toy, or even forming an organization such as a nation or a company.

In fact, everything that you want to do or have ever wanted to do has been a product of new or recycled information. By generating information, you are creating the conditions under which your life exists. The process of generating information and actualizing it is "Creation." You are a "Creator." Thus, you can create peace, by actualizing the information that you generate with your brain. A Power Brain can generate information that leads to peace.

On the physical plane, to activate the potential of your brain with Brain Respiration means to activate the senses of your body first. The body's sensory organs transmit what we see, hear, and feel to the brain, which recognizes and interprets the signals. Thus, when you feel something that you could not feel before, or see something you previously could not see, it signifies that both you senses and your brain have awakened to a fuller potential.

In a sense, we are using the body to awaken both the body and the brain. This is to awaken the body's senses and the brain simultaneously. We all have an established number of bodily movements that we use on a frequent basis. Consequently, our brain also records the patterns of those movements in its foremost circuits. Through a series of specifically designed exercises, including deep stretching and calisthenics, we can change the patterns of our movements. We use muscles that we do not normally use, thereby, breaking set patterns and stimulating both the body and brain to develop new awareness.

On an energetic plane, activating the potential of your brain means you allow your brain to "breathe" by supplying it with Ki-energy. More popularized in the West by the Chinese pronunciation of "Chi", Ki is the invisible energy that goes around and through all things in the universe, including us. Through the initial process of awakening our bodily senses, we experience a sensation unlike any we have had before. This is the sensation of the energy that is flowing through our body. The energy provides us with another medium or channel through which we can train our brain. Although our brain is composed of billions of nerve cells and controls the function of every other organ in the body, it cannot feel or even move itself. In the world of the five human senses, there is no way to consciously feel or move our brain. The only way that we can exercise or train our brain is to use a completely different medium from the physical. We can use a stream of Ki-energy and direct its flow to the areas in the brain that we wish to relax, exercise, or train. Increasing sensitivity to the energy is crucial and a basic requirement for the practice of Brain Respiration.

On a spiritual plane, Brain Respiration means nurturing the brain by feeding it good information. What is good information then? What are the standards by which we separate good information from bad information? Peace and Earth are ultimate yardsticks for determining whether a piece of information is good or not.

When faced with the need to determine the value of a certain piece of information, ask yourself, not whether this information will benefit me, my family, my company, my community, my country, or my religion, but whether this information is beneficial to my "Earth." Do not question whether the information will increase you personal success, ask whether it will help the process of peace. Earth and Peace are the keys to unlocking untapped potential of the brain. Our brain will perform at its highest level, in all three planes of existence, when we consciously recognize that peace and Earth are the two highest values in life.

A brain awakened to its full potential, with a healthy flow of energy and the ability to generate good information is a

Power Brain. A Power Brain is a brain of peace, and Brain Respiration is a way to develop Power Brains. As breathing through your lungs is good for your bodily health, Brain Respiration is good for your soul. Although our brain is the most elaborate and complex organ in our body, Brain Respiration is very simple and easy. The essence of Brain Respiration is learning to supply your brain with bright, positive energy and with good information on which to feed.

The Five Steps of Brain Respiration

Brain Respiration can be divided into five steps; Brain Sensitizing, Brain Softening, Brain Cleaning, Brain Re-wiring, and Brain Mastering. In relation to anatomy and functioning of the brain, these five steps begin with the body and work toward activation of every layer of the brain. During this process, the brain attunes to its ability to tap into the infinite life energy of the universe. From a spiritual point of view, Brain Respiration is a systematic way to realize enlightenment through everyday activity and behavior. From an educational point of view, Brain Respiration is a way to facilitate a life filled with emotional richness, harmonious relationships, life-giving energy, bright awareness, and a peaceful purpose in life.

The first step of Brain Respiration, "Brain Sensitizing," begins with reawakening the senses of the body, thereby shaking up the established patterns of the brain. Unlike other parts of our body, our brain is protected on all sides by a thick skull, thwarting any attempt, fortunately, to touch it from the outside. However, our brain connects to all parts of our body, controlling functions and registering complaints. Various parts of the body have corresponding areas in the brain that are in charge of control and feedback. The only way to "touch" and activate the brain is indirectly by stimulating different parts of the body. When our senses awaken and our concentration level increases, we are able to feel the subtle flow of energy that permeates our body. We can also stimulate the brain by directing the flow of this energy.

The second step of Brain Respiration is "Brain Softening", which introduces flexibility into the circuits of the brain that have been established according to repeated patterns of information or movement. By increasing flexibility of the brain circuits, this step of Brain Respiration facilitates communication among different parts of the brain and thereby increases operational efficiency.

The third step is "Brain Cleaning", a clearing process for the brain, in which we clear negative memories and corresponding emotions that clutter the brain. Most experiences are stored in the brain along with associated emotions. When an experience that is similar to a previous experience occurs, the original emotional energy becomes active, causing us react again in a similar way. Therefore, one experience can affect the way we react to similar experiences for years to come. In this step of Brain Respiration, we clear away the emotional debris of earlier, perhaps traumatic, experiences in order to be free to experience life with infinite possibilities, once again.

The fourth step, "Brain Re-wiring," is the step to open a channel of communication to the infinite source of universal energy and thereby awaken hidden capabilities of the brain. This process goes beyond the anatomical brain part of the brain called the neo-cortex, where higher cognitive functions are processed. It goes beyond the limbic system, where emotional and instinctive responses begin, and into the realm of cosmic life rhythm of the universe. The innate creativity of the neo-cortex activates during this process, riding on a current of infinite energy, with the brain acting as a conduit. The result is total integration of the myriad and previously disparate functions of the brain.

The fifth and final step of Brain Respiration, "Brain Mastering," makes us the true master of our own brain. Becoming the true master of our brain is being able to utilize one hundred percent of the creativity in the newly integrated brain. Since the brain is an organ that feeds and prospers on information, the key to utilizing it to its fullest potential, is to nurture it with a steady diet of good information, information that is fresh, delightful, and joyous – in a word, peaceful. This type of information comprises Vision. A bright and grand Vision will bring the brain alive in the fullest sense of the word. We are charging the brain with the energy of Vision.

A vision that has the power to awaken and move the brain has to be simple and clear enough to be understood not only intellectually, but also in the deepest parts of the body. Such a vision must also be realistic enough to be worth our time and effort, and subject to an exact and accurate analysis of the progress we are making toward the goal. However, it must also be powerful and visionary enough to tug at our deepest desire to achieve something for the good of our world. Our Vision must be to contribute constructively to Earth peace, for our divinity and our brain are both designed to work this way.

Health According to Bran Respiration

To be healthy in body and mind must signify more than a mere absence of disease. Absence of disease is just a starting point for the real meaning of health. According to Brain Respiration, health of body and mind signifies the ability to consciously use one hundred percent of the abilities and energy of the body and mind.

Recognition that, "my body is not me, but mine", and that "my mind is not me, but mine", is the basis for our definition of health. The body and mind are not ends in themselves, but superb vehicles through which we are able to realize the desire of our souls. Unless we use the body and mind to fulfill the needs of the soul, we are not using them healthily, no matter how well developed they may be. A tool works best when used for its intended purpose. When we use our body and mind to accomplish the work of the soul, we can say that they are healthy.

Individual health of body and mind is necessary for social health. When each individual has the capacity to fulfill his roles and responsibilities for the benefit of all, then society is healthy. To fulfill these roles and responsibilities, individuals must be capable, intelligent, and skillful. To maintain social health, they must cultivate relationships and create communities. Just as we need regular exercise, proper diet, and time to play in order to maintain proper physical health, there are three basic components to a healthy society. These are honesty, diligence, and a deep sense of responsibility. These three values form the ethical backbone of any healthy society.

Spiritual health is necessary for complete health. We can judge the state of our spiritual health by the following three criteria. First, do you recognize inner spirituality, or divinity, within yourself? Second, do you have a desire to work for the betterment for all? Third, do you have enough awareness to control and process the information in your brain? In other words, do you have a Power Brain?

Recognition of innate human spirituality is the most basic premise of spiritual health. That your body is not you but yours, and your mind is not you but yours... that you are more than the sum of mind and body, is the first step toward this recognition. Without recognizing the soul, there can be no spiritual growth. Desire to improve the world is the second aspect of spiritual health. This is natural once you have opened your eyes to your soul. Your soul inherently wants to realize its basic essence of peace and harmony. Finally, to be able to control the flow of information into your brain means having the ability to consciously refuse information that you do not want, and accept and utilize what you do want. It also means that you are able to away information that is impeding your soul's work. This gives you power to spiritually heal yourself and others.

When all of these elements come together, we realize that total health is a state in which we recognize the true purpose of life. Through awakening spiritually, we develop awareness to utilize one hundred percent of our physical and mental abilities and energy to realize our goals. Brain Respiration is truly a comprehensive system of health in which the practitioner, starting with the physical health (health), goes on to learn to use his mind in an expansive and bright fashion (happiness), subsequently realizing his own spirituality and purpose in life (enlightenment), then devotes himself to realizing his purpose in society, thereby bringing benefit to all (completion).

The process of Brain Respiration covers everything from physical health and inner happiness to spiritual enlightenment and completion of the soul. These do not occur in a vacuum, nor should they. They are painstakingly cultivated and achieved in relationship with others, based on honesty, diligence, and responsibility. Therefore, the Power Brain training process will also help heal society.

Brain Respiration helps you to experience the true reality of yourself. The essence of the Brain Respiration educational system is not study in the ordinary sense of the word, but more a recovery of the senses. The goal of Brain Respiration is to recover Yullyo, the natural rhythm of life that resides in humans and in all life. Yullyo is eternal life, light, sound, and vibration. I also call this Cosmic Energy (Chunjikiun) and

Cosmic Mind (Chunjimaeum). Yullyo is the beating and pulsing reality of all life. Brain Respiration is an experiential educational system that helps people to recover Yullyo, to establish harmonious relationship with each other and with nature, and ultimately, to become one with the grand harmony of Heaven, Earth, and Human. This is the essence of peace.

Qualification of a New Human

Full health is the most basic requirement for becoming a New Human. When I started the New Human movement I began by teaching calisthenics in a local park. However, even more important than a physically strong body is a correct relationship between the mind and the body.

The second requirement is social competence. You must be able to take care of your own basic needs before you can help others. Social competence is a combination of information and skills. You must acquire enough education and skill to be able to achieve the goals you have chosen for yourself.

The third requirement is a rich and stable emotional life. A New Human is able to exhibit a full range of emotions, and express them appropriately. When emotions have natural and healthy expression, you will be able to play well with others and with nature. A New Human is someone who plays well.

The forth requirement is to listen to your conscience. Conscience arises out of love of truth and desire to be truthful. Conscience is an expression of our perfect divinity within.

Because of our conscience, we instinctively seek to return to a state of integrity when we have lost it.

The fifth requirement is to become spiritual. Spirituality does not refer to super-human ability to see and hear unusual things. Spirit is information. Energy vibrations communicate information. When our brain has access to energy vibrations of spirit, we are "inspired". A person's level of divinity depends on the spiritual level of information he or she receives. To be divine is to receive and generate high quality information.

Our brain is open to all sorts of information and ideas. We choose what to accept and what to reject according to our habits and tastes. At the most basic level, it is a matter of the strength of our desire. From a bookstore full of countless types of books, we will base our selections on the strength of our desires. A spiritual person has a strong desire to benefit all of humankind, gathering and generating information toward that end. This is the life of a New Human, and the reason to develop a Power Brain.

Third Step

Peace through Enlightenment

~

M any people have romantic ideas about enlightenment. Many of them pursue enlightenment as a means of escape, chasing after dreams of eternal peace or freedom, or trying to escape real world suffering or difficulty that they feel unable to deal with. Such is not enlightenment.

Enlightenment has a definite purpose and goal. If you wish to surround yourself with a nebulous cloud of feel-good love and peace, then you harbor a huge misconception. People often think that enlightenment is an eternal state of peace and quiet. Perhaps in a metaphorical sense this is so, but you must not remain there for long. A child may be pure and innocent, but what power does a child have to change the world? Remaining in a state of isolated peace and quiet may be good for an individual, but is useless in bringing peace to the world. True enlightenment imparts wisdom and strength to effect positive change the real world. If enlightenment has no bearing upon the state of the real world, what good is it?

First, and foremost, enlightenment is a choice. Enlightenment is not the creation of a new state of being, but acknowledgement of something already existing within you. It is the recognition of your body and mind as instruments of your soul. Enlightenment is choosing to recognize that your soul is your true self, an integral part of the cosmic rhythm of life without beginning or end.

Enlightenment is rediscovering the principles of harmonious order within, and acknowledging that peace is the not only the highest, but the only real value that your soul can strive for. Enlightenment is freedom from preconceptions and real freedom to choose our values and beliefs. From this state of mind, we are free to act for the benefit of all. For the essence of the soul is peace, and the divinity within recognizes that are all One.

How can we arrive at enlightenment? The reason that we can arrive at enlightenment is that we have been given, from birth, all the conditions and equipped with all the tools necessary to reach such a state. These "tools and conditions" is the divinity within us, the perfect completeness of life that we all possess. We can refer to this perfect completeness as "bright mind," in Ancient Asian term. A sense of "Conscience" comes closest in meaning. Conscience is different from being legally right or wrong. Conscience has nothing to do with social norms or moral dictates from specific religious or spiritual dogma. Conscience is our conscious awareness of the divinity within, a perfect completeness of life that cannot be veiled or ignored. Through our sense of conscience, we realize when we are wrong, when we have lost our balance. Your sense of conscience is not a matter of effort – it has been given to you from birth. Enlightenment is a consciousness awareness of this state of your own life's perfect completeness; whether you acknowledge this state or not is your choice.

What is the purpose of enlightenment? Why do you seek to arrive at enlightenment? The purpose of enlightenment is not in itself – it is not a medal or an award that you receive. It is a matter of knowing why you exist – you are stepping up to the starting line of life. There is a huge difference between standing at the starting line and looking down towards the finish line and crossing the finish line itself. Enlightenment is a matter of standing at the starting line; it is not the finish itself.

Ultimately, no matter what kind of a race you run, the goal of life is the same. It is to achieve a completion of soul and realize peace within and without you. Realization of peace and spiritual completion go hand in hand, for our ultimate reality is peace. By realizing peace, you will have completed the journey of the soul – this is the one and only purpose of enlightenment.

Then, what is the way, the method to enlightenment? Enlightenment is a choice. And the best guide to enlightenment is the inner divinity that we hold. And the way that inner divinity can communicate with us is through our brain. Our divinity is in the brain, and our soul lies in our hearts. You can feel the truth of a situation through your heart, once you learn to open its senses. To love your brain, you feel your brain, you communicate with your brain – to love your heart, to listen to your heart, to communicate with your heart, such are the ways that you will be guided by the inner divinity. And Brain Respiration is a way to allow you to meet with this guide.

What are the results of enlightenment? Enlightenment refers to the discovery of the inner divinity that is peace and the recovery of the accompanying sense of harmony and creation. It is to throw off the yoke of the information and habits that have been controlling your life and recreate yourself anew with a new purpose in life. Your new identity and goals cannot be handed t your by someone else. You can only choose what you wish to do and become after you recover your sense of conscience. For me, my conscience told me to heal the society and the earth. The reason I chose healing is that it was the only choice available to me to live a truthful life.

Enlightenment is a choice, and healing is the actualization of that enlightenment.

If we cannot communicate enlightenment to others or use it to bring about a better world, then what good is that enlightenment? In business terms, if enlightenment were a product, I decided to test market it to target groups to see if they liked it. If they did like it and it became a success, then the product was a valid idea. I guess they liked it, since I am still here!

I am not smarter or better educated than others. However, I do know that what my soul wants is peace, and I know how to use the tools at hand, matter, energy, and information, to do its bidding. To not know something, is nothing to be afraid of, you merely lack information. However, you might well be afraid of knowing, and not acting on what you know, for then you are consciously forsaking your cosmic responsibility.

Enlightened Principle of Harmonious Living

More important than being enlightened is acting enlightened. What good is it to be at peace while the rest of the world is in shambles? Enlightened action shows that the principles of harmonious order have become an essential part of our thought process. We must then transform the principles of harmonious order into principles of harmonious living. Let us examine this further.

First, we will shift our focus from single-minded material success, to a desire for completion or perfection. Success comes with pursuit of fame and riches, but completion refers to knowing our purpose in life and doing our best to realize it. Success is a relative measure of our life's accomplishments, for we are comparing ourselves to what others have done. Completion is an absolute measure of accomplishment, as we measure ourselves, not against others but to own voice of divine conscience. Success requires us to compete against one

another in an endless race. Completion does not require competition, since we already have a winner's trophy reserved for
us as long as we finish the race. On the road of completion, the
more people that cross the finish line, the greater our joy. This
naturally leads to sense of camaraderie and cooperation. This
is in stark contrast to competition, where we are happy if our
neighbor falls down and is unable to finish the race.

Second, the underlying basis of human relationships will
no longer be one of control but one of mutual respect. This is
becomes possible when we recognize that the divinity that
exists within us, exists within all others. Just as we follow the
spiritual dictates of our conscience, so will others, promoting
an atmosphere of mutual and unconditional respect. A firm
belief in the divinity of others will compel people to treat each
other as they would treat heaven.

Third, the basis of our transactions will change from competition to cooperation. If we forsake our conscience for
personal gain, it is sad evidence that we have not yet recognized enlightenment. To be enlightened is to remain true to
our conscience, faithful to our divinity, and thus to our eternal
soul. On this basis, we will maintain mutual respect and the
right of each of us to a reasonable living.

Fourth, concept of ownership will change from possession
to stewardship. With enlightenment, we will realize that possession is an illusion that arises from attachment to a false
sense of security and permanence. Everything that is ours,
including our minds and bodies is on loan to us to facilitate
the growth of our soul. We are not actually owners, but

stewards, of what we think is ours. When we die, all we can take is profound satisfaction for the work we have done to improve the world during our lifetime. We cannot take material things with us, despite efforts of various rulers in the history of the human society!

Fifth, our concept of profit will change from that of personal gain to that public benefit. With enlightened awareness, we will not seek personal profit at the expense of the greater public good. We will realize personal benefit within the context of the public good. It will essentially be a "both...and" relationship instead of an "either...or" relationship, as it often is today.

Transformation of the basic concepts of transaction and profit will ease the fatal flaws in our current market system. The marketplace is a system in which different values come together and compromise reached. Supply and demand determines the worth of a product on the market. When a product is popular, its price goes up accordingly and we invest more money and effort into making the product even more popular. Such is the basic law of the market system. However, we are unable to explain certain phenomena that do not follow the supply and demand model and we are beginning to recognize the inherent limitations of our market system.

An underlying assumption of the market system is that every player is fully and equally informed of relevant information that could have a bearing on a given product. However, we know that such an assumption is unrealistic. A fatal flaw in the market system is that we cannot put a price on life's most basic values and therefore they are not available for transaction in the marketplace. Our current market system is neither mature enough to deal with such values, nor honest enough to acknowledge that they exist. We will only solve this inherent flaw with revolutionary evolution of our collective human consciousness.

In order for enlightenment to become a matter of common sense, we must base society on the principles of harmonious living. This will come about only when those who recognize their own enlightenment stand up and set an example of enlightened and harmonious living for others. When one hundred million New Humans declare themselves as such, the destiny of the Earth will change.

What Does Completion Mean?

Many spiritual minded people pursue "enlightenment" as their life's goal, wasting much time and effort. What they do not realize is that, on the road to spiritual completion, enlightenment is just a beginning, not an end in itself. Enlightenment is recognition of our innate divinity within, and acknowledgement that this is our true nature. Enlightenment is the result of a profound and brave choice to know ourselves as we truly are.

The important thing is not this "knowing" but acting. Life is precious precisely because we have the courage and the will to live our lives as we are supposed to live them, for peace for humanity. Life is precious precisely because it requires us to participate in its creation.

Significance of Spiritual Growth

We can use a computer analogy to explain the significance of spiritual growth. A computer process consists of hardware, software, and the user. Your soul is analogous to the user, your body to the hardware, and your mind, with all of your knowledge and information, to the software. Your soul provides the impetus, or desire, for spiritual growth, as the user decides what task to do on the computer. Just as we replace computer hardware when it wears out, our body regenerates on a regular basis. However, this does not mean that the user is changing. No, the user is the same and only the computer is new. As we upgrade software to a newer version, we receive newer and better information. One important distinction to keep in mind here is that as we upgrade the hardware and software, the user is growing and maturing throughout the process. The user, or soul, grows spiritually in the direction of eventual completion of Oneness with God, Cosmic Energy and Cosmic Mind. The computer hardware and software are merely tools for the user, for a certain task, which is completion of the soul through a spiritual growth process.

In order for the user to process higher quality and quantity of information necessary for growth of the self, he or she must upgrade the computer system. After all, you cannot expect to surf the web with an original IBM PC and two 5.25" disk drives with 16 RAM. This, in our lingo, means that you have to upgrade your brain to a Power Brain. As I previously stated, Brain Respiration is a way of upgrading the brain that I have found to be equally effective and applicable to almost everyone.

Three Studies Necessary to Complete Spiritual Growth

As long as your life's goal is completion of your soul, every moment and every situation is an opportunity to learn and grow. However, you may choose to consciously facilitate the process by pursuing these three studies. They are the Study of Principle, the Study of Practice, and the Study of Living. The Study of Principle is realization of the Truth, the Study of Practice is the process of incorporating the Truth into your body, and the Study of Living refers to actualizing the Truth in everyday life. Through these studies, your soul will mature and eventually reach completion. They are concrete, precise, and to the point. The prerequisites most needed for these studies are not innate intelligence, money, or special abilities. They are honesty, diligence, and responsibility. No one can complete these studies for you.

The first and the most fundamental of these studies is the Study of the Principle of harmonious order, which we have already discussed. The essence of this study is to recognize the reality of whom you are, to know that you are Cosmic Energy and Cosmic Mind, and to acknowledge harmony within you. You cannot accomplish this by reading books.

The second is the Study of Practice or training. This study consists of training yourself to make your actions consistent with what you know to be true. By imprinting acknowledgement of enlightenment into every cell of your body, you become actual embodiment of the divine conscience within you. Endless information, in the form of habits and memories, resides in our bodies and brains. We are born with some of this information and we accumulate more along the way. Other people impose much information on us without our explicit permission. The Study of Practice means that we are reclaiming our original purity by eradicating harmful information. Thus, we become an embodiment of the principle of harmonious order.

Third is the Study of Living, in which you practice enlightenment in your everyday life. Why do we need to do this? Why is meditating on mountaintops no longer enough? The reason we need this practice is to be able to measure the growth of our soul. The soul is invisible to the eye. So how can you tell how much it has grown? Observe your character, it is an accurate reflection of the maturity of your soul. We establish character through the process of interacting with others. During this process we make choices, are judged by them, reflect upon others' judgments, and adjust ourselves accordingly. Although this is sometimes a painful process, it is an opportunity to nurture virtuous and harmonious character. Since we can only do this by co-existing with others, the Study of Living is crucial. The purpose of this study is to transform the principle of harmonious order into a principle of harmonious living.

Three Methods to Help with Your Second Study

Although, strictly speaking, everything you do for spiritual growth is the Study of Practice, traditional Eastern spiritual practice has delineated three specific methods to facilitate the journey through this part of the process. We call these JiGam, JoShik, and KeumChok.

JiGam, means to "Stop-Emotion". It is a method used to train your mind to be clear and peaceful, uninfluenced by the winds of feeling and emotion. If you close your eyes for a second and listen to the chatter of your mind, you will realize just how busy, noisy, and jumbled it is. These noises of the mind, these thoughts that create emotions, go around in circles and do not go away just because you want them to. Conversely, the more you try to eliminate them, the louder they yell and the faster they move.

The only way to silence this noise of the mind is to find a center on which to focus, a shelter from the winds of thoughts, emotions, and other distractions. There are many training regimens for spiritual growth. The practice of yoga seeks to balance body and mind with specific physical positions. Zen Meditation pursues a calm mind by concentrating on a single nonsensical question designed to slow or stop rational thought. Asceticism also seeks release from constant chatter through purposeful suffering. These are all attempts to discover a point on which to center peace and calm of mind. However, a limitation of such trainings is they require extraordinary concentration and physical stamina, not suitable for everyday life in the real world.

In Brain Respiration (BR), we utilize the body's Ki-energy to reach this state of JiGam. Ki-energy flows continuously in, through, and outside of the body. When we can palpably feel the sensation of Ki-energy flowing through our bodies, our brain waves have fallen below the Alpha wave stage. In other words, this is a stage where thoughts and emotions are calm. By concentrating to feel the sensation of energy, we can approach this stage of calm more easily.

Starting with the hands, which are especially sensitive to energy, we first feel, and then gather energy into the lower chakra point, or dahnjon, in Korean. This allows us to approach a state of centered calm without little effort. This is when training actually begins. Most of us think that our thoughts and emotions are who we are. This is patently false. Thoughts and emotions are mere waves on the ocean of our true selves. We can only see what our true selves look like when the waves stop churning and the water is calm. This is the reason why we practice JiGam.

JoShik, means "controlled breathing", when directly translated. Because life energy travels through the body on trails of the breath, we can control the flow of energy, including its strength and underlying character, by regulating our breath.

The fact that we are able to control the flow of Ki-energy indicates that we can control the currents of our thoughts and emotions. This being the case, not only are we immune to the winds of thoughts and emotions, we are able to control the direction and strength of such winds. Through a simple thing like breathing, we are able to increase health of body and peace of mind, regulate flow of Ki-energy, and even control the mind according to our will.

However, the possibilities of the breath do not stop here. With continuous, deep, and sincere breathing, we will eventually meet deeper aspects of breathing, the cycle of the harmony of life. Breath is a concrete and immediate expression of life, an endless in... and out, that defines the harmonious cycle of life. With each breath we inhale, we are one with our body, ever grateful for this vessel of life. With each breath we exhale, we become one with the enveloping atmosphere, imbued with intense appreciation for the heavens. As we immerse ourselves deeper in our breathing, we become breath itself, neither inside nor outside, and without boundary. Although we breathe naturally from the moment of birth, the meaning of breath becomes deeper, without limitation, once we understand its significance.

There are three different methods of Brain Respiration for working with and controlling energy and breath. These are JiGam, HangGong, and UnKiShimGong. JiGam is training to develop sensitivity to energy through relaxed concentration. HangGong uses breath to gather energy into the body, and UnKiShimGong teaches the practitioner to utilize the flow of energy through the body, and to regulate thoughts and emotions, and thereby control the mind.

The final method to help you with the Study of Practice is KeumChok, which translates directly as "stop contact." Contact of outside stimuli with the five basic sense organs, the eyes, ears, tongue, nose, and skin, triggers thoughts and emotions. KeumChok means to stop the flow of information through the five senses. Turning the senses off is only possible when we are deep in a non-conscious state, often called "SunJungSamMae" in Ancient Korean. Here, you cut off all stimuli from outside sources, and concentrate awareness fully on your inner self, enabling you to meet a deeper reality of life.

In terms of brain structure, this is to go beyond the realm of control of the neo-cortex, and even the limbic system. It is to enter into the realm of the brain stem, which sustains basic life functions including breathing and beating of the heart. This is the realm where the harmonious cycle of life manifests within our physical body. When awareness approaches the brain stem, and merges consciously or unconsciously with the flow of energy that feeds it, we can affect the most basic functions of life. At this level, we can affect our autonomic nervous system and generate "superhuman" strength and "miraculous" healings. We can tap into an infinite source of energy though the brain stem, and use it for limitless creativity and energy, for peace for ourselves, and for society.

Using these three methods, you will be able to complete the Study of Practice, the second stage in the study of spiritual growth. Through this, you will become an embodiment of the principle of harmonious order by imprinting knowledge of enlightenment into every cell of your being. These methods will help you to move from the stage of "knowledge" to "knowing", where knowledge becomes conviction forged by training and personal experience. This is the difference between theory and practice, between reading a book on swimming, and swimming in a pool. It is the difference between reading about enlightenment and practicing it.

Ancient Philosophy of Enlightenment, the Heavenly Code

According to "HanDanGoGi" one of the oldest surviving history texts of Ancient Asia, the Heavenly Code, or "ChunBuKyung", dates back more than 9,000 years. It was first put into writing approximately 6,000 years ago using a form of writing that resembles a pattern of deer hoof prints. Transcription into ancient Asian calligraphy took place around 4,400 years ago, during the Ancient Chosen era. This was to be the first country recognized as precursor to modern Korea and Manchuria. This version was translated and recorded into modern Chinese calligraphy by Chiwon Choi, foremost scholar of the Shilla Kingdom of Korea's Three Kingdom Era around 1,200 years ago.

Although it known as the "Heavenly Code," it is not a religious text as it does not mention god(s) or outline a partic- ular dogma. It is possible to interpret the Heavenly Code in countless ways, yet all interpretations contain the following three basic truths about the cosmos.

First, everything begins with the One, and returns to the One, which has no beginning or end. Second, the One expresses itself as Heaven, Earth, and Human, all existing within the Human Being. Third, the Oneness of all must naturally express itself in actions that benefit all. In 2,334 BC, the kingdom of the Ancient Chosen called their kings Dangun. The Danguns interpreted the Heavenly Code as instruction to "Widely Benefit All Humanity" and "Rightfully Harmonize All the World," designating it as the philosophical and political foundation of the kingdom.

"Widely Benefit All Humanity, Rightfully Harmonize All the World", while serving as a guideline for the education of its citizens, also served as the political philosophy of an entire country for over 2,000 years. This provides proof that it is possible to facilitate the realization of spiritual enlightenment through a deliberately designed social and political system, rather than to leave it to individuals to discover by themselves. Ancient Chosen's history is the record of a country's successful attempt to base social, political, and economic principles on the Principle of Harmonious Order. This enabled actualization of enlightenment through harmonious living, woven throughout the fabric of their society. These three stages of enlightened social development were called, "JoHwa (Harmonizing)," "KyoHwa (Educating)," and "ChiHwa (Governing)," respectively.

A society of this nature provides her citizens with the best possible environment for completion of the soul. By being born into this society, you would automatically be enlightened to your true self and your true objective in life. You would undertake completion of your soul by accomplishing your life's goals, and perfect the cycle of harmonious order by helping others along the journey. The point I am making is that we can design the social and educational system of a country to teach her citizens the principles of harmonious living transcending race, religion, and nationally. If we can all agree on an optimally constructive and beneficial model of society for all of humanity, this will be the shape of a real, equitable, and lasting peace.

Below, I have included the original Chinese ideogram of the Heavenly Code and a literal translation of meaning. The Heavenly Code explains how to use our God given right to enlightenment to realize peace on Earth.

We may interpret the Heavenly Code as an exercise in mathematics, philosophy, or even the study of energy. Each letter of the Heavenly Code contains its own distinct letter or numerical meaning when read and energy/musical characteristics when sounded. This combines the effect of numbers/ratios, and sound/energy characteristics of individual components to create a holistic effect, as an actual representation of the Principle of Harmonious Order that it records. Thus, the Heavenly Code itself is Harmonious Order. This is Yullyo for Yul means a numerical ratio and Lyo means rhythm. Therefore, Yullyo is a cosmic system of numbers expressed as rhythm. This is Cosmic Harmony. This is Peace.

天符經

Heavenly Code

一始無始一析三極無
盡本天一一地一二人
一三一積十鉅無匱化
三天二三地二三人二
三大三合六生七八九
運三四成環五七一妙
衍萬往萬來用變不動
本本心本太陽昂明人
中天地一一終無終一

The essence of ChunBuKyung lies in the phrase, "In Joong Chun Ji Il," which signifies that the heaven, earth and human are all connected in the Oneness. This Oneness is defined as a beginning without a beginning and end without an end, a point out of which all came from and will go back to. This Oneness is expressed by the character "Il," meaning One.

一始無始 (Il She Mu She)
One Begins Unmoved Moving, That Has No Beginning

一析三極無盡本 (Il Suk Sahm Guk Mu Jin Bohn)
One Divides To Three Crowns, While Remaining A Limitless Mover

天一一地一二人一三 (Chun Il Il Ji Il Ee In Il Sahm)
Heaven Comes First, Earth Comes Second, Human Comes Third

一積十鉅無匱化三 (Il Juk Ship Guh Mu Gweh Hwa Sahm)
One Gathers To Build Ten, And Infinite Forms Become The Trinity
(of heaven, earth, human)

天二三地二三人二三 (Chun Ee Sahm Ji Ee Sahm In Ee Sahm) Heaven Gains Two To Make Three, Earth Gains Two To Make Three, Human Gains Two To Make Three

大三合六生七八九運 (Dae Sahm Hahp Yook Saeng Chil Pahl Goo Une) Three Trinities Make Six, And They Create Seven, And Eight, Nine Appears, And There Comes A Turning

三四成環五七一 (Sahm Sah Sung Hwan Oh Chil Il)

Three And Four Form A Circle, Five With Seven Makes One Whole

妙衍萬汪萬來用變不動本

(Myo Yeon Mahn Wang Mahn Lae Yong Byun Bu Dong Bon)

Way-Less Is The Way All Comes And All Goes, Features Are Changing, And Change-Less Is The Maker

本心本太陽昂明 (Bon Shim Bon Tae Yang Ahng Myung)

Divine Mind Is Eternal Light, Looking Toward Celestial Light

人中天地一 (In Joong Chun Ji Il)

Human Bears Heaven And Earth, And The Three Make One

一終無終一 (Il Jong Mu Jong Il)

One Is The End Of All, And The One Has No Ending

If you had to reduce all 81 letters of the ChunBuKyung into 1 letter, it would have to be "Il." "Il" refers to One – One in Korean is called "Han." "Han" refers to the source of all existence. "Han" describes the breath of the cosmos, the endless cycle of inhaling and exhaling of the process of creation and life. To know and experience this endlessness is the goal of every religious and spiritual tradition.

On a social level, this "Han" is the center point of all order and the basis of all value judgments. It is an alternative to the obsessive outward material expansion based upon competition and conflict, an alternative that will lead us away from the duality system that we live in into a system of trinity.

Fourth Step

Peace through Healing Society

~

The chief structures of the human value system to this point have been nation, religion, and ethnicity. These have caused an endless cycle of war and conflict in the name of freedom, justice, and peace for individual groups. The freedom, justice, and peace gained from these wars are prejudicial by nature, focused on the needs of only one group, and achieved at the expense of another group or groups.

The horrific terrorist acts of September 11, 2001 have shown us that our sense of security, our economic prosperity and military strength will not save us from harm. Who would have thought that the most powerful nation in the history of the world, both militarily and economically, would be vulnerable to such acts of wanton destruction? We now have no choice but examine the nature of our "pursuit of peace". Is it truly effective, and is it truly for peace? As our old value system begins to fail, will we continue to fulfill only our individual needs by competition and domination, without regard to the whole? Can we not find collective values, and share a collective dream? Is this the best that we can do? Is this really what we want? These are the questions we must ask and answer.

Both our intellect and our deeper spiritual wisdom tell us that this is not so. My joy is your joy, my soul is our soul, and my destiny and our destiny are not mutually exclusive but inherently interdependent. Perhaps we can all revolve around the sun as one, united entity.

It is imperative that we find a shared standard of value to overcome differences in our various human societies. We must find a central and comprehensive system of living values that will unite humanity while preserving and even celebrating diversity. We must learn to 'rotate' individually while we 'revolve' collectively. Where can we find such a common standard?

This must be the earth.

The Earth, the root of our existence, is the central value that we all share. No truth that we seek, or values we live by can exist without the Earth. Even our particular gods cannot exist without the Earth. In Neil Gaiman's exquisite novel American Gods, a buffalo-man symbolizing the land is referring to the gods when he says, " ...they never understood that they are here – and that the people who worship them are here – because it suits us that they are here - but we can change our minds… and perhaps we will." Everything owes its existence to the earth. Without Earth, we are nothing.

Any philosophy or ideology that claims peace is its highest ideal, yet fails to recognize Earth as humanity's common denominator, will eventually collide with another philosophy or ideology that also claims that peace is its highest ideal. This is because they both derive from the position of a particular religion or nation. Without a central, common ground by which to define peace, peace will elude us. This central common ground can only be the earth. Nothing, within our realm of experience, can exist without it. Only Earth can become the rallying point for a realistic plan for lasting peace.

Life is a trip, not only in a metaphorical sense, but literally. We are all taking a trip around the universe on a spaceship called, Earth. Our souls dropped onto the fertile plains of Earth and we became passengers in human bodies, not knowing our point of origin or our destination. It is as if we have been unknowing participants in a cosmic bungee jump. What we must realize, however, is that this trip is a journey for growth of our individual souls, and for the collective soul of humanity. We can get there only if we go together.

Our souls are clamoring not for a "separate peace" that belongs a particular religion, nation, or people, dividing us into losers and winners, but for an "Earthly peace" that can be celebrated by all life on Earth. True peace will come when we all realize that Earth is the final arbitrator of life, and that Earth-Human is our highest common identification as human beings.

Earth-Humans

An Earth-Human is someone who realizes that Earth, and peace on Earth, are the central standards, by which we should measure all decisions. How can you know if you are making the right decision for the Earth? Just follow your conscience, for it is part of the soul of the Earth and the Cosmos. If our conscience stands for that divine scale within us, by which to judge the relative weight of options that face us, then the point on the scale that corresponds to zero is Earth. By calibrating our inner scales to the Earth, we are making Earth the standard by which to judge our options. In other words, Earth is the absolute value against which we may judge all other relative values.

Many people claim to love the Earth. However, what exactly does that mean? Just as loving home does not refer only to caring for the house, loving the Earth cannot be limited to environmental protection. Loving the Earth must include acknowledging her people as one unified community. We must then protect our home and our entire family. This is what loving the Earth can mean.

An Earth-Human has a connection to body, mind, and energy of the Earth. An Earth-Human knows he or she is one with the earth, and one with the whole of humanity. He or she therefore cares for and heals neighbors and family members with the unconditional love of the soul. An Earth-Human is a healer in every sense of the word. When our consciousness makes the leap and becomes Earth consciousness, we gain strength and wisdom to overcome the small boundaries of self and group-egotism, and feel love for all of life on Earth.

Some people argue that we should not limit awareness to the Earth in this age of space travel and space stations. What they do not realize is that being truly aware of the Earth will allow us to gain awareness of the cosmos as well, for they are intimately interrelated. They are in fact, one. You will experience cosmic awareness when you become truly conscious of the Earth. To do so, you must be free of preconceptions and self-defeating ideas of limitation. Earth provides us with a matrix for the path to conscious evolution and cosmic awareness.

Just as Earth is a tiny part of the universe, humanity is only a small segment of life on Earth, despite our grand illusions. However, it is significant when even one person increases consciousness enough to feel the wholeness of Earth in his or her heart. When that person recognizes the Oneness that connects all of life in a web of vibrant energy... that one person will see the Earth, and life, as "home," with a feeling of love and protection that home generates.

This is the amazing power of increasing consciousness, the profound result of enlightenment. Even more amazing is that as human beings, we possess enlightenment from birth. We merely have to choose to become aware of the cosmic vastness of our own consciousness.

The first words spoken to a newborn baby should be, "Welcome to Earth. You are an Earth-Human, whose life's roots are buried deep in the heart of the Earth." This should the very first thing we teach a child. This should be the first message the human brain receives, for it is the highest form of enlightenment there is. Despite the obviousness, people do not realize the Earth is the foundation of their life. Nations and religions exist because of the Earth. Even space travel, as we know it, exists because of the Earth. However, schools do not teach this. A curriculum that explains the relationship between Earth and humanity is yet to be developed. If we were to realize the true meaning of Earth and Earth-Human, it would be impossible to hate each other as we do.

We did not come to Earth to compete against one another as separate entities. We came Earth to found a peaceful global community, centered on the Earth. Only we can bring about world peace. Earth-Humans, who see the reality of the Earth as a community of life interwoven, can bring harmony to the world. Earth-Humans go beyond the boundaries of nation and religion with expanded awareness, recognizing the fleeting nature of artificial separation that so limits us. In time, we will no longer belong to one particular people, country, or religion. We will all belong to the Earth.

The Earth-Human Movement: Healing Society

To heal humanity and the Earth there must be a world wide, socio-cultural movement that goes beyond the sphere of individual intentions and good deeds. Earth-Humans must be the driving force behind this movement. This is our Vision. We must join with many others on this path... for our Vision will require the gifts of many. We must overcome prejudice, and work with people from all cultural, national, and social backgrounds to make our Vision a reality. Earth-Humans will be the leaders of the long overdue movement to establish lasting peace on Earth.

Healing Society Movement, or the Earth-Human Movement, is a socio-cultural movement based upon our collective realization of our enlightenment, expressing it in terms of our love for the earth and the humanity and realizing health for the community and the society. Health does not refer to the physical health alone, but to the physical, mental, social, and spiritual health – when all these four dimensions of health are achieved can we say that we are healthy. I started this movement twenty years ago in a small, local park, teaching Brain Respiration calisthenics to one person – now it is being taught in over 3,000 place in Korea, in addition to centers in the USA, Europe, and Japan. However, my original aim remains true: to heal this society and the world.

There are many aspects to healing. On the level of the individual, healing means to recover lost physical and mental health. This is to facilitate free and unimpeded flow of life energy to the body, and to restore original brightness and purity to the soul by nurturing it with hope and courage. Healing society means that after individuals attain health and enlightenment, they help each other on the journey of completion of the soul.

Healing the Earth means to establish equitable and lasting peace, for benefit of all people of the world and for Earth herself.

An important part of healing society is to heal the family, for families make up the smallest and yet the most essential unit of society. Healthy families are necessary to the health of society, and humanity. Parents must assume responsibility for health of the family. They must help children understand who they are and to find their purpose in life. Parents must convey to children, their inalienable right to enlightenment. Parents who are Earth-Humans will teach them what it truly means to be a citizen of the Earth.

Parents must be healers for the family. I am not speaking merely about healing physical ailments, but the caring and accepting attitude of love. All that is required to be a healer is to facilitate a deep level of trust among family members. When we communicate trust in the world, peace will be possible. Conflict in the world today is fundamentally due to the lack of trust.

Parents also have responsibility to make the family a joyful unit. To stay together, a family must play together. Without a playful atmosphere, there can be little communication between parents and children. We must be able to play well not only with each other but also in society, and in nature. Healing is creating an atmosphere in which to play well, for when we are having fun, we do not fight.

Peace though a Spiritual United Nations (the SUN)

~

Human civilization is essentially externally driven. "Stronger, higher, and faster" is not only the aim at the Olympics, is the thrust of human civilization. This kind of external motivation inevitably results greed and conflict. The result is our current civilization, which is obviously in crisis.

We must shift to a civilization in which Earth is the center of all "living" values, and by which we can overcome our differences in social and cultural values. We must create a civilization in which Earth-Humans are the principle actors and in which we live by the principle of harmonious living. We must create a civilization in which all people realize that their true purpose in life is to nurture their soul, and in which all people can be creative, productive, and peaceful. We need a New Human civilization founded on the concept of "Universal Benefit to All Humanity – Rightful Harmony to all the World."

What should we call this new civilization? I choose to call it a Spiritual Civilization, to emphasize our understanding of the limitations of a purely material civilization. This new civilization will not reject material things, nor give up the notion of technological and material advancement. However, we will define growth and maturity in a new way. Spiritual civilization does not stand on the opposite shore from material civilization. It encompasses and surpasses the great successes of the latter.

Where should we begin and with what? If we were to try to change the entire infrastructure at once, stress alone would probably destroy civilization. How can we turn the bus around without an abrupt stop that would throw everything inside the bus into chaos? What has to happen to create a fundamental change?

The philosophy on Earth must become one of "HongIkInGan and EWhaSaeGue". In Korean, it means "Universal benefit to all humanity, rightful harmony throughout the world." It refers to the desire benefit the world, not as a demand, but a choice. The Earth-Human concept is relevant to the paradigm shift that our world requires today. In historical context, it is rediscovery of what it means to be human. It could even be the first recognition ever, of what it means to be human, for no civilization that we know of, has achieved such a momentous shift. It indicates our willingness to accept absolute responsibility for our choices regarding our future. Knowing that the future of the Earth depends us, we have chosen to accept the challenge.

By identifying ourselves as Earth-Humans, a series of changes in our way of life will have to follow. We will need to shift from a non-sustainable to sustainable civilization, from a civilization that worships the material, to a civilization that uses material wisely. From a civilization defined by winning and losing to a civilization desiring completion of the souls of her people.

We must also shift from being a hypocritical civilization in which ideals and reality conflict, to being an honest and conscientious one in which life is an accurate reflection of the love in our hearts. We must change from a self-destructive civilization to a self-nurturing civilization. We will change from being in a world of Russians, Arabs, Americans, and Africans, to being in a world of Earth-Humans... from a world of Christians, Buddhists, Hindus, and Muslims to a world of inner spirituality.

From civilization that cannot even safely dispose of its own garbage, to a mature civilization that will pick up what it has dropped, replant where it has harvested, and put back what it has taken. From a foolish civilization where history endlessly repeats itself, to a wise civilization that realizes that the Heaven, Earth, and Human are the basis of all existence.

We will have a civilization in which individuals accept responsibility to actualize the bright light of enlightenment within each of us. We will change from a world where people live in inner isolation and fear in a sea of information, to a world where all people of the Earth will communicate freely and understand each other.

To many people, this sounds like an impossible dream. However, this is not a matter of reinventing the wheel but a matter of turning the steering wheel of the bus. It depends entirely on us.

Let us begin by awakening our dormant senses first. We do not lack for information. What we lack are our senses that should warn us of the gravity of the situation we are facing right now. When we have awakened these senses, we can begin the transformation. Let us all awaken the senses that will allow us to communicate with each other and with the Earth in a way that verbal language cannot. Let us awaken the sensation of energy that gives us life, and the spirit that is our eternal existence.

Enlightenment is not far away. It could not be closer. Stop putting your own enlightenment off and choose to acknowledge it – this is the first step. This choice will bring you clear-sightedness to see the world as it really is, and to honestly judge what you have done so far. It will show you where you want to go in the future.

Education develops character in humans. Thus, the educational system should be the first thing that is changed. Parents must once again take on the role of educators, enlightened educators who can communicate their Earth-Human awareness to their children. An Earth-Human parent is a teacher, healer, and an activist at home. They are healers skillful enough to care for their family's mental and spiritual health, and activists who live what they teach. When parents fulfill their roles as teachers, healers, and activists, homes will compel society to recover its lost role as a living, vibrant community. Change at home will translate to change other parts of society. Home will be a rich and fertile field from which the seeds of Earth-wide change will sprout.

Peace through the SUN: The Vision of 2010

World peace is just a term that expresses hope. It is not an actual vision or strategy that can be put into effect. Without a concrete vision or goal, energy, ideas, and wisdom do not come together to focus on a single problem. Even if they do, it is only temporary, for nothing binds them.

Peaceology is not just a conceptual philosophy, but philosophy for action. It is an attempt to cultivate a tree of peace in the field of truth. Peaceology would be an empty concept without the concrete vision that I hope to see actualized by the end of the decade.

An Earth-wide change is obviously beyond the realm of any individual or family unit. An Earth-wide change is likewise impossible for any one organization or country to effect, no matter how large or strong. It is only possible for a world wide spiritual alliance of Earth-Humans to transcend religious, national and ethnic affiliations. Although we do not yet have such an organization, when there is one, I would like to call it the SUN.

SUN stands for the Spiritual Union of New Humans, an association of New Humans who have chosen to actualize their acknowledged enlightenment by healing humanity and the Earth. We need one hundred million people in every corner of the world, to rise up and declare themselves New Humans. They will form a network of people whose highest common identification is as Earth-Humans, throwing off the noose of ethnicity, religious affiliation, and nationality that has been slowly choking us for the last few thousand years. These one hundred million Earth-Humans will awaken the rest of the world with the roar of their collective shout for joy as the rope falls from their necks. This process of creating a worldwide culture for harmonious living is the deepest form of healing.

It is our goal to have 36,000 healing educational centers by 2010. These healing education centers all over the world will offer people the philosophical, technological, and educational resources needed to establish a new civilization. They will provide a model of Earth-Human living suited to the various regions of the world where the centers are located.

The SUN is a Spiritual Union of NGO's, an alliance of non-governmental organizations that are going beyond political and territorial barriers, to realize love for humanity and love for Earth. NGO's will no longer work separately from each other as they pursue particular issues that relate to the health of the Earth, such as the environment, debt-relief, immunization, conflict resolution, etc... While each NGO will retain its own specialty, their battles, set-backs, and triumphs will be shared by every other group in the SUN who will offer support, guidance, and influence to realize the goals of each member NGO within the greater goal of peace.

The SUN is also a Spiritual Union of Nations, an alliance of nations that acknowledge that we are all Earth-Humans despite our differences. The governments of these nations will understand that they cannot continue to make policies that seek to benefit their own citizens at the expense of world citizens. The governments of these nations will officially acknowledge that any actions taken by one nation could affect any other nation. These governments will write into their constitutions the solemn promise that they will take into account the interests of the Earth and the whole of humanity before making policy decisions.

Ultimately, the SUN is the Spiritual United Nations, a complimentary organization to the international and mainly political existing United Nations. SUN will support the UN's original goal of the eradication of the disease of war and become active in the promotion of cultural and non-political activities designed to bring people together.

The SUN is this and more. It is the sun to brighten and warm the new spiritual civilization. SUN is not just the birth of another organization, for civilization will not change just because we register a new organization, appoint board members, and adopt new by-laws. Humans have to change in a fundamental way, or nothing will happen. Our living values must change, our attitude toward life must change, and the basic nature of our desires and ambition must change, from outer to inner, from external to internal, and from winning to perfecting. When the SUN becomes reality, it will be representative of the new value system, new character, and new way of life of the Earth-Human.

If only one percent of the Earth's population chooses to live for the future, and chooses to undergo a personal shift, then Earth's destiny will change. Most studies indicate that Earth's population will reach ten billion in the near future. We need only one hundred million Earth-Humans to pioneer a shift in civilization. If we combine our strength and focus our power of enlightened vision on the SUN, we will effect a true change and kick the door to the future wide open. This is what I envision for next ten years with Peaceology, Brain Respiration and the Healing Society Movement... and with one hundred million partners in peace.

Humanity Conference:
The Declaration of Humanity

~

World-renowned scholars, thinkers and social activists gathered together in Seoul, Korea in June of 2001 to explore the concrete influence that spirituality can have on political, economic and cultural makeup. Dr. Ilchi Lee, Neale Donald Walsch, Seymour Topping, Maurice Strong, Jean Houston and Al Gore were among the distinguished guests.

The primary result of the conference was adoption of an historic Declaration of Humanity, a brief document that states the intention of Earth-Humans to establish a peaceful world community. The declaration was officially adopted by distinguished guests, conference participants, and more than twelve thousand other enthusiastic Earth-Humans. To date, more than one hundred thousand people have signed this declaration.

Declaration of Humanity
June 15th, 2001

1. I declare that I am a spiritual being, an essential and eternal part of the Soul of Humanity, one and indivisible.
2. I declare that I am a human being, whose rights and security ultimately depend on assuring the human rights of all people of Earth.
3. I declare that I am a child of the earth, with the will and awareness to work for goals that benefit the entire community of earth on Earth.
4. I declare that I am healer, with the power and purpose to heal the many forms of divisions and conflicts that exist on Earth.
5. I declare that I am a protector, with the knowledge and responsibility to help Earth recover her natural harmony and beauty.
6. I declare that I am an activist in service to the world, with the commitment and the ability to make a positive difference in my society.

If you would like to sign your name as a sign of support and agreement, please visit www.healingsociety.org.